PROBLEM SOLVING

AND
PROGRAMMING
IN **TURING**

First Edition

J. N. P. HUME

Holt Software Associates Inc.

Publisher:
HOLT SOFTWARE ASSOCIATES Inc.
203 College Street, Suite 305
Toronto, Canada M5T 1P9
(416) 978-6476

ISBN 0-921598-16-5

First Edition

Printed in Canada by the University of Toronto Press

Table of Contents

APPENDICES

Preface

Computer Programming is approximately forty years old and **problem solving** (both as concept and goal) has been with us since the beginning.

In the past one of the common difficulties with problem solving-based computer science textbooks was that problem solving was often very much subjugated to programming language issues. Other textbooks tended to select a single systematic way of creating a computer program, usually by the step-by-step refinement technique, and apply it throughout the book to all programs.

In **Problem Solving and Programming in Turing**, however, I have tried to create a text in which problem solving is much more than a servant of computer programming. Rather, I have tried to use computer programming as a means of illustrating various problem solving techniques. (This means that chapter headings that are a normal part of a book dedicated to computer programming do not appear. For example, searching and sorting is spread over several chapters that have titles concerning problem solving methods.)

I have tried to organize the sections in a useful and intuitive manner. In each chapter I have attempted to build successively on the concepts learned from previous chapters. It is important to note however, that individual teachers may have other preferences and so may wish to deal with the chapters in a different order.

I have also attempted to pose problems that all students can relate to. I have begun the book with arithmetic problems because here the idea of abstraction appears most naturally, for example, that $2 + 2 = 4$. It is not my intention though, to push the solution of mathematical problems as the only way to approach the subject. Graphics-based problems are just as demanding and intriguing Programs that produce graphical output also have a great appeal for students and provide a natural way of involving them and encouraging then to learn new skills in their search for the most dynamic graphic.

In **Problem Solving and Programming in Turing,** graphics, in the form of character graphics, are used as soon as the notion of repetition is introduced. Pixel graphics comes a little later.

For each chapter I have included an "Errors You Might Make" section, in hopes of assisting students to identify possible areas of difficulty, and thus save them from frustration. Students should be encouraged toward careful reading of this section to ensure that they recognize that these are mistakes to be **avoided**.

Some effort has also been taken to provide information for students in a readable, straightforward, and friendly manner. The sections have been laid out with easy-to-find subject headings. The "Table of Contents" and the "Index" will help all readers find specific information. A "Glossary of Technical Terms" has also been provided to help students with the subject vocabulary. The language of the text has been directed at the average high school student. My goal here was to make it as clear and readable as possible without over simplifying the material. It should be noted, however, that students with language difficulties may require additional assistance.

Computer science has undergone many changes in the last forty years, and of all subject areas that we teach, it is perhaps the most fluid and hence interesting. The development of new programming languages like Turing have allowed us to progress from spaghetti programs that were unstructured, error prone, and unmanageable to structured programs with proper control constructs. With these improvements, programs are no longer labyrinths of control. As teachers, this means that we are now free to concentrate on the important ideas of computer science.

Now it is time to marry the power of the computer to the human activity of problem solving. And that is what I have tried to do in this book.

J.N. Patterson Hume
University of Toronto

Acknowledgments

Writing a book is a daunting task. I was encouraged to launch on the project by Chris Stephenson whose contact with many high school teachers told her what kind of book was really wanted. Chris read every word, corrected copy, supervised layout and design, and pressed me to meet all deadlines. Ric Holt devised the illustrations on his Mac. Tom West tested the example programs and compiled the index. Inge Weber entered the text and patiently modified it over and over. Annemarie Polis designed the cover and title page. All these were part of the terrific team from the publisher.

But great credit goes to the high-school teachers who agreed to review the preliminary edition and provide us with front-end feedback.

Their criticisms and suggestions were extremely valuable and resulted in important changes and additions to the book. But most of all their enthusiasm for the presentation was extremely heartening. My thanks to these:

Glenn Boisvert (Owen Sound C.V.I.)
Myra Darling (Emery C.I.)
Brian Garcia (Lester B. Pearson C.I.)
Jon Grandfield (Bracebridge and Muskoka Lakes S.S.)
Martha Greenhow (Emery C.I.)
Greg Hoggarth (The Country Day School)
David Kempton (Sutton D.H.S.)
Brian Kennedy (Seaforth D.H.S.)
Joe Kolarich (Sacred Heart)
Dennis Lafontaine (Central Elgin C.I.)
George Leibold (Glenforest S.S.)
Tony Lopez (Orangeville D.S.S.)
Steve MacDonell (Madonna C.H.S.)
Ed O'Brien (General Vanier S.S.)
Ihor Orenchuck (Stratford Northwestern)
Doug Peterson (Essex County Board of Education)
Bernie Pickett (St. Mary's H.S.)
Valerie Radford (Red Lake D.H.S.)
Peter Richardson (Tilbury D.H.S.)
David Riegert (Pickering H.S.)
Cam Samuel (Westview Centennial S.S.)
Cindy Schroeder (Manhattan H.S.)

Arie Spiering (Pickering H.S.)
Dwight Stead (Cardinal Leger S.S.)
Sal Trabona (Madonna C.H.S.)
Dan Witt (St. Mary's H.S.)
Freda Zomer (John Paul II)

J.N.P. Hume

Chapter 1

PROBLEM SOLVING:
A MAP OF THE TERRITORY

*Problem solving is many things
to many people.*

Whenever you set out to explore a new area of knowledge it is a good idea to have a sense of the size of the area and to have some general notion about the different parts of it.

It is the same as setting out on a trip. You need a map of the territory that you will be traveling in.

Problem solving is many things to many people.

In this introductory chapter we will try to describe the limits that we are putting on the area to be explored.

The problems that we will look at will be in the realm of **logical** problems. A different area of problem solving involves **design** problems, the kind you would meet as an architect, an artist, or an inventor, for example.

The solution of logical problems is a very small part of the universe of problem solving. But we hope the experience with this small part will help you when you go into new uncharted regions.

Questions and Answers about Problem Solving

Q.   What is problem solving?

A.   Problem solving is the process of finding certain information that is not known from a set of information that is known.

Q.   How do you know that you want to know this certain information that you do not know?

A.   Someone has to pose this to me as a request or a problem. They specify what is known and they ask me to find out certain things that are not known.

Q.   Do they always give you exactly the amount of information I need to find out what they want to know?

A.   Usually in problems posed to me in textbooks that is the case.

Q.   What if they give you too little information?

A.   Then I cannot find a solution unless I make up the missing pieces of information myself.

Q.   Can you make up anything you want to?

A.   I would try to make up something that was reasonable and then say to the person posing the problem: "I have assumed such and such information which was not in the specification".

Q.   Does that solve the problem?

A.   It solves *a* problem and it may be satisfactory to the problem poser. There are many possible solutions to the problem as specified.

Q.   Is there sometimes too much information supplied in the problem specification?

A.   There are two possibilities. Either the extra information is really just a repeat of other information, that is, it is redundant; or the pieces supplied are inconsistent and there is no possible solution.

Q.   Are problems with redundant information really just the same as ones with exactly the amount you need?

A.   Yes.

Well-Posed Problems

We will begin by looking at a very simple problem:

Sarah was born in 1980. How old will she be in 1995?

You probably would just answer 15. And you would be right. But how did you do it? What is important is to begin at the beginning and observe what is going on in the process of problem solving. In this way you can see a pattern emerging. In the problem specification you are told certain information; this is what is **known** to you. In this case, Sarah's year of birth and the year you want to know her age. Then you are asked to deduce certain information, that is the **unknown**. You are asked her age in 1995.

You find the value of the unknown by examining the **relationship** between the unknown and the knowns.

To express this relationship we need to have names for the unknowns and the knowns.

The knowns we will call *birth year* and the *present year*. The unknown we will call the *age in present year*. We can now write a relationship, namely

age in present year = present year − birth year

Now we can substitute numbers in this **formal** relationship.

age in present year = 1995 − 1980 = 15

So we conclude that Sarah's age in the present year is 15.

The problem is solved once you can express the relationship formally. Sometimes in science we speak of formal relationships like this as being a **formula**, and we memorize a whole lot of formulas. Solving problems then just becomes a matter of substituting values into a formula.

In the formula or relationship to solve for an unknown, we must write it in a way that has the unknown all by itself on the left-hand side of the equation.

What if we had this problem to solve?

Sarah will be 15 in 1995. What year was she born?

It is really the same problem but what is known and unknown is different. You would rewrite the formal relationship this way

birth year = present year – age in present year

Substituting numbers you get

birth year = 1995 – 15 = 1980

Problems like this are very common in mathematics or science.

Because the way you write the formal relationship is different depending on what is known and what is unknown, some people think you must memorize several formulas. You should know how to express any one of the relationships and then be able to rewrite it in different forms.

Problems

Here are some well-posed problems. Write a formal relationship between the knowns and unknowns and then substitute values.

1.   Hong's mother was born in 1942. He was born in 1968. How old was his mother when he was born?

2.   Sasha works every Saturday in the grocery store as a check-out cashier for $68.00. She saves her money. How much will she have saved after 50 weeks? (We will not include any bank interest.)

3.   Rachael deposits $300.00 in her saving account. How much will she have at the end of one year if the interest rate is 7% per annum (year)?

4.   A bank pays 5% interest per year on savings in a year when the inflation rate is 1.8%. What is the real rate of return on saved money?

5.   Yannis bought a skate board and paid a total of $85.21 including the sales tax of 15%. What was the price of the board before tax?

6.   The inflation rates for the last three successive years are 4.2%, 3.1%, and 1.7%. What is the equivalent price to-day for a movie ticket that you paid $5.00 for three years ago?

Calculators and Computers

When your problem solving efforts require you to substitute values in a formal relationship, it is often helpful to have a calculator. Before calculators were so inexpensive to own, many people worked everything out using pencil and paper. This meant that they had to be good at arithmetic. Very often problems in textbooks were posed with very simple numbers so the hand calculations would not be difficult. After all, the important thing was to know how to solve the problem, not to carry out the arithmetic.

Now there does not need to be any attempt to keep the values simple. With a calculator one set of numbers is as easy as another. This means the problem can often be more realistic.

Computers carry the idea even further. They provide a still more powerful tool to help in solving problems. A computer is especially useful when you need to carry out repetitious calculations as it can save you from spending hours with a hand calculator.

The development of tools to help us has broadened our horizons about problem solving. Problems that were nearly impossible before are now routinely solved using the computer.

- Before computers were used to work out school timetables it was virtually impossible to offer a variety of optional subjects to students.

- Airlines could not book seats without long delays.

- Banks could not possibly have had daily interest accounts.

- Credit card purchases could not be rapidly validated.

Problem Solving and Computer Programming

To take advantage of the power of computers in solving problems it is essential to understand what they can and can not do and how you might go about using them. One of the best ways to begin to understand how computers can be of use is to learn to write programs. Most of you will not become computer programmers but it will be the rare person who will live in the twenty-first century who does not use computers one way or another.

Computer programming and problem solving are excellent companions in a course of study. Many problems have already been solved and the solutions to these problems has led to the developlment of many different kinds of computer programs that perform specific jobs or sets of jobs. These are **application programs**.

- For example, there are many **text processing programs** that let you enter things like essays and letters, file them for future use, edit them, set them in different type sizes and **fonts**, and **format** them for publication. These are the basis of **desk top publishing**.

- Other commonly used application programs provide easy ways to prepare financial plans, like budgets. They are called **spread sheet programs** because the information is usually spread out in rows and columns for easy reference.

- A third very common application program maintains files of information in the computer, such as student files kept by a school. This data is indexed so that you can access any particular individual record in the file or all records that have certain characteristics, such as all students studying computer programming. This is called a **data base program**.

Some courses about computers introduce these three types of application programs as well as of the technical terms that you need to know to use them. Using application programs is not really computer programming. The question is why should anyone learn programming itself when knowing how to run an application lets you use the computer.

Computer Programming and Systematics

In learning how to solve problems it is important to be conscious of the system that you are using. It is only by being systematic that we can build our ability to solve new problems. This is the very foundation of science, being systematic – organizing our knowledge. We are constantly building on the work of others, not just accumulating a lot of disorganized facts.

Preparing a computer program to solve a problem requires you to be systematic and precise. What is more, a program that is less than correct is no use at all. You must refine it until it is perfect.

Of course, nobody is perfect. When you first prepare a program it might produce crazy answers. You must correct the **program errors** until it gives correct results on the **test data** that you feed it. And you must try to give it a wide enough range of test data so that you will be sure it always gives correct results. Otherwise it is useless.

Fortunately, our computers have systems that help you in producing correct programs. They can spot a lot of common errors and give you **error messages**.

In many of the chapters we have listed common programming **errors that you might make**. These lists should help you to find your errors or perhaps avoid them in the first place.

There is a great satisfaction in getting things right. And satisfaction in being able to express your instructions to the computer precisely.

All of this enhances your problem solving ability: using the computer as a tool, but also being able to express your own systematized knowledge.

How to Begin

This book tries to present to you the systematics of problem solving and the systematics of computer programming. Sometimes the emphasis will be on the practical details of using a computer. At other times we will be stressing the problem-solving aspects.

No study of this pair would be meaningful without problems to be solved and a computer on which to solve them. We will assume that you have access to a microcomputer (**hardware**) and that the computer has stored in it the programs (**software**) that will let you program in the language that we will present, namely the Turing programming language.

The Editor

In order to be able to put your programs into the computer, edit them, run them, and save them, there must be what is called an **editor**. This editor is slightly different depending on whether you are using a PC microcomputer, or a Macintosh microcomputer, or an Icon microcomputer. There are three versions of the next chapter. You need only read one of these depending on which kind of microcomputer you have. After that, everything is very nearly the same and you may proceed to the rest of the chapters.

Questions and Answers

In each chapter, even this one, we have included a series of questions and answers. These are meant to be read by you. They answer some preliminary questions, sometimes forming a review of things you should already know. They should prepare you for the later sections of the chapter

Technical Terms

At the end of each chapter is a list of words that have special meaning for problem solving and computer programming. It is a good idea to check to see that you have a reasonable understanding of each term. You should, in fact, be able to explain in your own words what each means. In Appendix 7 there is a glossary giving the meaning of many of these terms.

Problems and Questions for Discussion

In each chapter there will be **problems** for you to solve. The ones with a more pure mathematical character are marked with an asterisk.

Questions for discussion are included in each chapter. These provide a chance for you to clarify your understanding of certain ideas.

Often a discussion of problems is good, before you start to work them out in detail. In many companies today, software is written by groups of people, each person contributing her or his abilities and input. Working in groups in the classroom is an excellent way to help clarify your ideas. Often, when you are stuck, someone else in your group will have a good idea. The method of **brainstorming** has been used successfully where you just contribute ideas from the "top of your head" and then criticize them as being sensible or not. You should not be afraid to speak out for fear of being wrong – or laughed at.

Another method of problem solving called **lateral thinking** encourages you to approach a solution sideways rather than head on. Sometimes this starts you off on a new train of thought which might lead to an original solution.

In general the method we will be using is one that moves somewhat more systematically. As we said at the beginning of the chapter "Problem solving is many things to many people".

Questions for Discussion

1.   In many textbooks there are answers in the back of the book to problems. Does that mean the problems are well posed?

2.   You are asked to design a system in your school for fire drill so that the school could be evacuated in the shortest possible time. Is this a well–specified problem? What would you need to know?

3.   What are the knowns and the unknowns in a crossword puzzle?

4.   Have you ever read anything about brainstorming or lateral thinking as methods for solving problems?

Technical Terms you should now know

known

unknown

redundant information

formal relationship

formula

calculator

computer

application program

text processing

type font

format

desk top publishing

spread sheet

data base

systematics

program error

test data

error message

hardware

software

editor

brainstorming

lateral thinking

THE EDITOR FOR THE PC

*In the editor we can enter
the program, correct any errors we
make in typing, and then run it.*

In order to be able to enter a Turing program into the computer we need to use the **editor**.

In the editor we can enter the program, correct any errors we make in typing, and then run it.

To do this we make use of special **commands** that are not part of the Turing programming language. They are called **operating system** commands.

Some commands are given by selecting them from a **menu** of possible commands.

To select a menu command we first press the **alt** key which changes us to the menu command selection mode.

Other commands are achieved by using special keys: the arrow key, the **Del** (delete) key, the **Ins** (insert) key, or the **ctrl** (control) key.

Note:

If you are using a version of Turing that uses the line editor (any version previous to 7.0) you will find a description of the editor in Chapter 2C.

The Turing Environment

- When you begin a session on your IBM compatible personal computer you should be in the Turing Environment. (If you are in the operating system of the PC, type the word *turing* then press the Enter key.) In the Turing Environment you will see a window, called the **program window**, filling almost the entire screen.

- At the top in the **title bar** of the window is the word *untitled*.

- Above the window there are a number of words:

    File   Edit   Search   Run

- These are called the **menu bar** and form the categories for a number of commands that you can give.

- At the upper-left corner of the program window is a blinking underline. This is the **cursor** and indicates where what you type on the **keyboard** will appear in the program window.

- The cursor may be moved around in the window by pressing the **arrow keys** on the right-hand side of the keyboard.

Typing in the Program Window

Move the cursor so that it is near the middle of the screen then type "this is fun". Now see if you can type "THIS IS FUN" right below your first line. Move the cursor first to where you want to start typing, then hold down a **shift key** (there is one on either the lower left or the right side of the standard typewriter keys marked by a fat up-arrow) and type the **upper case** or **capital** letters.

When you are typing one line after another it is convenient to use the **Return** key, the one with the crooked left arrow just to the right of the standard typewriter keys. When you press Return the cursor moves down one line and right over to the left side of the window.

Editing What You Have Typed

So far you see how to enter text into the window. One of the great things about computers is that you can change what you have entered very easily; you can **edit** the text.

The Turing Environment provides a simple word processor. You could, if you wanted to, use it for essays or letters. We will use it for entering Turing programs or preparing data for our programs.

- If you mistype a letter, or any **character** such as an asterisk, you can backup one space (by pressing the **backspace** key) and then type the correct character. The original character is erased when you do this.

- You can **delete** characters already typed by moving the cursor (using the arrow key) to the first character you want to delete and then pressing the **Del** (delete) key for each character you want deleted.

- To **insert** characters, move the cursor to the character that is to follow the insertion and type the insertion. As you type, the characters on the same line following the insertion move over to make room.

- Practice editing by changing you text from "this is fun" to "They say this is easy".

Selecting a Menu Command

- To give a command we must move the cursor to the menu bar. To do this press the **alt** key. The cursor is now at the first item on the left, which is the **File** menu heading. The word **File** is highlighted and below it appears the list of commands that are in the **File menu**. These are **New, Open, Save, Save As, Print,** and **Exit.**

- You can **select** a particular command from this menu by pressing the down arrow until the command you want is highlighted. You then press the **Return** key to have the selected command executed.

- Another way to execute the command that is displayed in the current menu, is to type the character or press the key that is highlighted or appears after the command name.

- You can move to other menus than the **File** menu by pressing the right arrow key.

Saving What You Have Typed on the Disk

*   To save what you have typed in the program window on the disk you would select **Save As...** from the **File** menu.

*   When you choose a command that has three dots after its name more information is needed before it can be executed.

*   When you press Return a box appears on the screen. This is called a **dialog box** because it asks you to enter the name that you want to give to the disk file that will store what is in the program window.

*   The cursor is positioned in the dialog box so that you can type the disk file name, then press Return.

*   When you do this, the top of the window will show this name rather than the word *untitled*. The disk will give a whirring sound and your file will be recorded there.

*   You should have your own disk and remove it from the computer when you are finished with a session.

Your Computer Disk

*   In order to use a disk it must be **formatted** so that information such as programs or data can be stored on it. We assume that you have received such a formatted disk from your instructor.

*   Be careful how you handle it. When you put it in the disk drive do not force it. Keep it clean, dry, and away from heat or magnets.

*   When you begin a session at the computer and want to bring a file that is on your disk into the program window, so you can edit it, select the **Open...** command from the **File** menu.

- When you do, a box appears showing the list of the names of all the files that you have saved. This is the **directory** of files.

- The cursor is pointing at the first file name in the directory list and the name is highlighted. You can move it from name to name using the arrow keys. The name currently being pointed to is highlighted.

- To open the highlighted file, press Return. The file will appear in the program window and its name will be at the top of the window.

Running a Turing Program

- When you finish typing a Turing program into the program window, you can run it by selecting the **Run** command from the **Run** menu. The program window and the menu bar will disappear and the whole screen becomes the **execution** or **input/output window**. It will display the results of running: the output of the program and a record of anything you type during its execution.

- If you have an error in your Turing program, an error message will appear at the bottom of the window. If you press Return you will be returned to the program window. The cursor will be at the point in the program where the error occurred and a description of the error will be at the bottom of the screen.

- You can correct the error by insertion or deletion.

- If there is more than one error you can find the next error by selecting the **Find Next Error** command from the **Search** menu.

- After errors are corrected you can run the program again.

Starting a New Program

- To start a new program with a blank program window, you should save your present program then choose **New** from the **File** menu.

- A dialog box will appear asking whether or not you want to save the current program. You type *y* (yes) or *n* (no). If you have not saved the program and you type no, the program will be lost!

- To stop execution of an executing program, press **control-break** (Hold **control** key down and press the Pause/Break key) On PC systems where **control-break** has been disabled (such as AN/ICLAS), one can press **control-B** instead (Hold **control** key down and press B).

- To end a session using Turing, select the **Exit** command from the **File** menu. You will be returned to the PC operating system (DOS). You can then log off the computer.

An Example Turing Program

Here is a program for you to type in and store on the disk.

```
% The "times" program
% Outputs a multiplication table
var number: int
put "Choose a number between 1 and 12 " ..
get number
put "Here is the multiplication table for ", number
for i: 1 .. 12
    put i: 2, " times ", number, " is ", i * number: 2
end for
```

Save the program as a file called *times*. Now select the **Run** command. When the prompting line

Choose a number between 1 and 12 _

appears in the I/O window you should then type a number between 1 and 12 inclusive. When you finish typing press Return or the computer will not know you have finished. As soon as you do, the multiplication table will appear for the number you have chosen. The number you type is shown here in white. Here is a sample output screen:

```
         Choose a number between 1 and 12 6
         Here is the multiplication table for 6
             1 times 6 is   6
             2 times 6 is  12
             3 times 6 is  18
             4 times 6 is  24
             5 times 6 is  30
             6 times 6 is  36
             7 times 6 is  42
             8 times 6 is  48
             9 times 6 is  56
            10 times 6 is  60
            11 times 6 is  66
            12 times 6 is  72
```

Suppose you wanted to have a table showing your number multiplied by the values 1 to 20 rather than 1 to 12. What change in the program might do this? Try changing it then run it again. Store the changed program under a new file name, say *times20*.

Try changing the program by substituting a / for the * in the program. You will have a division table instead of a multiplication table. Can you fix the rest of the program to suit this change? Store this program as *divide* on the disk.

Here is a slightly longer program. When it is in the window, give the **Run** command and play the guessing game. After you have played the game try reading the program to see if you can understand some of it even before you have learned anything about the Turing language. Here is the program:

```
% The "number" program
% Chooses a number at random between 1 and 99
% and allows you to guess it
var hidden, guess: int
var reply: string(1)
put "See if you can guess the hidden number"
put "It is between 1 and 99 inclusive"
loop
    var count: int := 0
    put "Do you want to play? Answer y or n " ..
    get reply
    exit when reply = "n"
    % Choose a random number between 1 and 99
    randint (hidden, 1, 99)
    loop
        put "Enter your guess ",
            "(any number between 1 and 99) " ..
        get guess
        count := count + 1
        if guess < hidden then
            put "You are low"
        elsif guess > hidden then
            put "You are high"
        else
            put "You got it in ", count, " guesses"
            exit
        end if
    end loop
end loop
```

Save the program on the disk as *number*.

Menus of Commands

Here is a summary of the various commands available in the Turing Environment

File	Edit	Search	Run
New	Cut	Find...	Run
Open...	Copy	Find Next	Run with Arguments...
Save	Paste	Find Next Error	Paragraph
Save As...	Clear	Change...	
Print			
Exit			

Problems

1.   Clear the program window, then enter a short letter to your teacher telling her or him how exciting it is to be using the computer as a simple word processor. Print the letter if you have a printer. Store the letter on the disk under the file name *teacher*. Check the directory to see that it is there. The program window can be used to enter any kind of data.

2.   Change the letter you wrote for question 1 so that an extra paragraph is added about how simple it is to edit text on a computer. Arrange to send this same letter to a friend as well as to your teacher. Print both new letters if you have a printer. Store them as files called *teacher2* and *friend*. Check the directory to see that all three files are there.

3.   Here is a Turing program to type into the program window and run

```
% The "seesaw" program
% Makes saw tooth patterns
loop
    put "How many teeth do you want? (1–12) "
    var count: int
    get count
    put repeat (" *         " , count)
    put repeat ("   *     * " , count)
    put repeat ("     * *   " , count)
    put repeat ("       *   " , count)
end loop
```

Try running the program. If you get tired of making saw tooth patterns you can stop the execution of the program by selecting **Stop** from the **Run** menu.

Selecting Text in the Program Window

Cutting and **pasting** are terms that describe ways to move text from one place to another in a computer document. Cutting and pasting make it much easier to edit a program.

To perform these operations, you must be able to **select** a portion of the text that is to be cut.

Suppose that you wanted to select a word in the text. Place the cursor at the beginning of the word, press the **shift** key and holding it down move the cursor to the end of the word that is to be selected. The word is highlighted. It will remain highlighted until you select some other part of the text or select the **Clear** command from the **Edit** menu.

To select a whole paragraph you can press arrow keys so that you go from the beginning of the first word (top-left corner of the paragraph) to the end of the last, at the bottom-right corner. This move can be made diagonally across the paragraph.

Using a Mouse

If you have a mouse you can use it to position the cursor, select menu commands, or select text for editing.

- To position the cursor, move the mouse so the cursor is in the desired position and **click** the mouse button.

- To select a menu command, place the cursor on the menu heading and pressing and holding the mouse button down, **drag** the mouse down the menu until the command you want is highlighted. Then release the button.

- To select text, move the cursor to the start of the text then, pressing the mouse button, drag to the end of text to be selected. You can select a passage of text by dragging diagonally from the beginning to the end of the passage.

Editing the Program using Menu Commands

- If, after you have selected text, you choose the **Cut** command from the **Edit** menu, the selected text will disappear.

- If you want it to reappear, give the **Paste** command from the **Edit** menu.

- When text is cut it is stored on the **clipboard**.

- When the **Paste** command is given, the clipboard's contents are inserted wherever the cursor is currently located. By moving the cursor after giving a **Cut** command, you can paste text into any location you want.

- Pasting does not erase the clipboard so you can paste the same text as many times as you like.

- Selected text can be copied onto the clipboard and not deleted (cut) from its present location by giving the **Copy** command from the **Edit** menu.

- Any **Cut** or **Copy** command will erase the previous contents of the clipboard and then place the currently selected text there.

NOTE:

The next sections describe features of the editor that are more advanced and can be referred to later.

Searching for and Replacing Text

To find the occurrence of a particular word in a text, choose the **Find...** command from the **Search** menu When you do, a dialog box appears asking you to type in the text you are searching for. When you type this in and press **Return**, the first occurrence of the sought for text following the cursor's current position is highlighted and the cursor moved to it.

If you wanted to change it you could use the usual editing methods to do so. If you know that you want to change one word to another you would choose the **Change...** command from the **Search** menu. The dialog box asks you what word (or words) you want to replace and what you want to replace it (them) with.

To continue to do the same replacement on a sequence of occurrences you can use the **Change...** command again, leaving the same set of words in the dialog box.

Redirecting Output to a Disk File

If you wanted to save the output of a program on a disk file, you should choose the **Run Arguments...** command from the **Run** menu.

A dialog box appears asking you what you want to redirect: the input or output. When you indicate which, a second dialog box asks you to name the disk file where you want the output to be saved.

Input Data from a Disk File

If you want to have the input of program come from a disk file instead of from the keyboard, choose the **Run with Arguments...** command from the **Run** menu. Select input redirection and then fill in the name of the input file in the dialog box that appears.

Printing a Program or its Output

To print a program that is in the window you can choose the **Print** command from the **File** menu. You can paragraph your program in the standard Turing style before you print by choosing the **Paragraph** command from the **Run** menu.

To print the result of execution, you must redirect the output to a disk file. This file can then be opened in the program window and printed as a program.

You can also print output by redirecting it to a file named *printer*.

Technical Terms you should now know

Turing environment
program window
title bar
menu bar
command
cursor
keyboard
arrow key
shift key
upper case
capital
Return key
edit
character
backspace key
delete
Del key
insert
File menu
New command
Open... command
Save command
Save As... command
Print command
Exit command
Selecting a command
Saving a file
dialog box
formatted disk
disk drive

directory of files
highlighted
Run menu
Run command
execution window
input/output window
error message
Find Next Error command
Search menu
New command
ctrl-c
log off
shift key
selecting text
Clear command
mouse
mouse button
clicking mouse
dragging mouse
Cut command
clipboard
Paste command
Copy command
Find... command
Change... command
Run with Arguments...
    command
redirecting output to disk
redirecting input from disk
printer

THE EDITOR FOR THE MACINTOSH

. . . all Macintosh applications look similar.
Once you have learned how to use one,
others are easy to learn.

The Apple Macintosh differs from other personal computers in having a built-in **toolbox** of software in a read-only memory (ROM).

These tools can be used by authors of other software applications. This means that all Macintosh applications look similar. Once you have learned how to use one, others are easy to learn

All applications involve a device for communicating with the computer called a **mouse**, as well as the usual keyboard

When you start up the computer, the screen displays a **bar** of **menu titles** across the top.

Below the menu bar is an area called the **desk top** containing **icons** (little sketches) representing the available information: programs and data.

The Turing Environment

When the Turing system has been activated on the Macintosh computer, windows appear at various times on the screen:

- **program window** for inputting your Turing program

- **I/O window** (or **execution window**) for displaying what data you input and what is output by the computer

- **error message window** for displaying notices about errors in your program

- **dialog boxes** for requesting more information from you in response to certain **commands** that you have selected from the menu of commands.

The Mouse

The mouse is a small plastic box that fits neatly into your hand. It has a wire connecting it to the computer. On the bottom is a ball that can be revolved by rolling the mouse on a table top. As the ball is revolved a **pointer** moves on the screen. In this way you can point to anything on the screen, for example, a menu or an icon.

On the top of the mouse is a button that can be pressed. If you press down then release the button in quick succession you are **clicking** the mouse. If you do this twice quickly you are **double clicking**. If you press down you are **pressing**; if you press, and without releasing it, move the mouse pointer by rolling on the table, you are **dragging** the mouse. These basic mouse manoeuvers are essential to operating the Macintosh.

Startup Procedure

- To start up your Macintosh: turn on the power and wait until an icon appears on the screen showing a computer with a question mark on its screen.

- If you have a hard disk drive, the Turing System will be loaded on it and the Turing icon will appear. You can skip to the section *Using the Turing System.*

- If you do not have a hard disk drive, you insert a **startup disk** which contains the basic system software under which all application programs run. Disks are inserted label side up with the metal end first. Again you wait. Notice that the mouse pointer changes to a wristwatch icon whenever you must wait.

- Next appears the startup desktop display with its menu bar across the top. On the desk top is a disk icon labelled **System Disk** and a garbage can icon labelled **Trash**.

Selecting a Menu Command

- You can see what menu items are available under a particular menu title by moving the mouse pointer to that title in the menu bar and pressing. When you do this the whole menu of commands under that title appears.

- You can select a particular command from this menu by dragging down the menu to that item, then releasing the mouse button. Commands that are not available for selection at any particular time are displayed in grey rather than black type. As you drag down a menu the command that you are currently pointing to is **highlighted**; it is displayed as white on a black background rather than as black on white. You can then easily see which command you will get if you release the mouse button.

Using the Turing System

- When the Turing icon is displayed you can open it by double clicking.

- When you do, you enter the Turing environment. The menu title bar changes to read, after the apple symbol: File, Edit, Search, Window, and Run. Also a window labelled **Untitled** appears in the upper left half of the screen. This is the **program window**; a flashing vertical line at the top left of the window, the cursor, shows where anything you type will go.

- You can change the position of the cursor to any point in the window by pointing at that position using the mouse, and clicking. When the mouse pointer is in an active window its icon changes from an arrow pointer to an I-shaped pointer. This can be positioned precisely, for example, between letters you have already typed.

- You can now type in your Turing program. The keyboard is similar to a standard typewriter.

- By pressing the backspace key (or delete), at the upper right, a letter just typed can be deleted.

- You can delete at any place by moving the cursor to the space following the deletion and backspacing as many times as required.

- To insert extra characters, simply move the cursor to where you want to insert and type the insertion. When you finish, move the cursor elsewhere, using the mouse.

- A Turing program can be paragraphed in the standard Turing style by selecting the **Paragraph** command from the **Run** menu.

Printing or Saving the Program or Input/Output

- To be printed, a window must be the **active** window. This is signified by the horizontal lines in the title bar of the window. Just select **Print** from the **File** menu.

- To make another window active just click anywhere inside it.

- You can also save the active window by choosing **Save As**... from the **File** menu. A dialog box will appear asking you to provide the name of the file where the window's contents are to be saved.

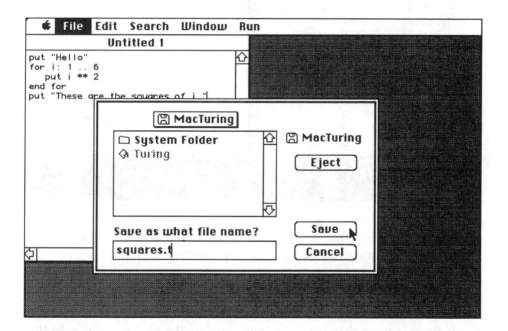

Running a Turing Program

- When you finish typing a Turing program into the program window you can run it by selecting the **Run** command from the **Run** menu. A second window will appear on the upper right of the screen. This is the execution or I/O window. It will display the results of running: the output from the program and a record of anything you type during its execution.

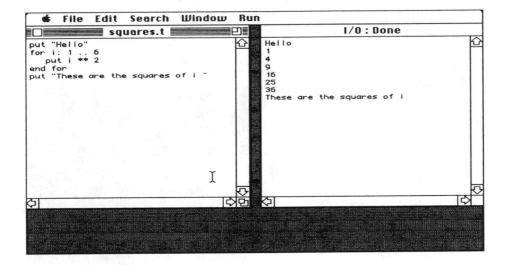

- If you have an error in your Turing program, an error message will appear in a window at the bottom of the screen describing the error. The line of your program where the error occurs will also be highlighted.

- You can correct the error by insertion and deletion.

- If there is more than one error, you can find the next error by selecting the **Find Next Error** command from the **Search** menu.

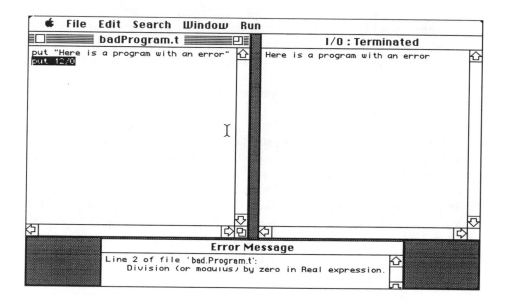

- After errors are corrected you can run the program again.

- The title bar of the execution window always indicates what has happened. It says "I/O: Done" if the program runs to completion. If it is interrupted due to an error that must be corrected, it says so. It stops if there is an error during execution or if you interrupt execution by selecting **Stop.** Selecting**Run** in the **Run** menu during execution causes the program to restart execution.

Starting a New Program

- To start a new program with a blank program window you should save your present program then choose **Close** from the **File** menu.

- If you have not saved the current program you will get a dialog box asking whether or not you want to save it. Click the response button you want (yes or no).

- If there are still windows open on the screen, you can close them by clicking in the small box at their upper left-hand corner. This is called the **close box**. Now select **New** from the **File** menu.

- If you want to see a program you have already saved on the disk, select **Open**... from the **File** menu.

- Whenever you choose a command that has dots after it a dialogue box will appear. You must give the required information before the command can be executed.

- In this case you will get a list of all the programs you have saved. This list is called a **directory**. Select the program you want to open by clicking on the little box beside its name. Its name is then highlighted. Now click the open button. (Alternatively double clicking on the name opens it right away.)

- If the directory of all your files does not display everything there is at one time, you can scroll the list in its display window by clicking the scroll arrows in the right border of the window. This is true of scrolling in any window such as the program or execution window when there is too much to be displayed all at once. Experiment with these scroll arrows.

- To end a session of using Turing select **Quit** from the **File** menu. This returns you to the original desk top. Now select **Eject** from the **File** menu. Your disk will be ejected from the disk drive and you can then turn off the power to the Macintosh.

An Example Turing Program

Here is a program for you to type in and store on the disk.

```
% The "times" program
% Outputs a multiplication table
var number: int
put "Choose a number between 1 and 10 " ..
get number
put "Here is the multiplication table for ", number
for i: 1 .. 10
    put i: 2, " times ", number, " is ", i * number: 2
end for
```

Save the program as a file called *times*. Now select the **Run** command. When the prompting line

Choose a number between 1 and 10 |

appears in the I/O window its title bar will say "I/O: Input expected". You should then type a number between 1 and 10 inclusive. When you finish typing press Return or the computer will not know you have finished. As soon as you do, the multiplication table will appear for the number you have chosen.

Here is a sample output screen:

```
          Choose a number between 1 and 10 6
          Here is the multiplication table for 6
              1 times 6 is  6
              2 times 6 is 12
              3 times 6 is 18
              4 times 6 is 24
              5 times 6 is 30
              6 times 6 is 36
              7 times 6 is 42
              8 times 6 is 48
              9 times 6 is 56
             10 times 6 is 60
```

Suppose you wanted to have a table showing your number multiplied by the values 1 to 20 rather than 1 to 10. What change in the program might do this? Try changing it then run it again. Store the changed program under a new file name, say *times20*.

Try changing the program by substituting a / for the * in the program. You will have a division table instead of a multiplication table. Can you fix the rest of the program to suit this change? Store this program as *divide* on the disk.

Here is a slightly longer program. When it is in the window, give the **Run** command and play the guessing game. After you have played the game try reading the program to see if you can understand some of it even before you have learned anything about the Turing language.

Here is the program:

```
% The "number" program
% Chooses a number at random between 1 and 99
% and allows you to guess it
var hidden, guess: int
var reply: string(1)
put "See if you can guess the hidden number"
put "It is between 1 and 99 inclusive"
loop
    var count: int := 0
    put "Do you want to play? Answer y or n " ..
    get reply
    exit when reply = "n"
    % Choose a random number between 1 and 99
    randint (hidden, 1, 99)
    loop
        put "Enter your guess ",
            "(any number between 1 and 99) " ..
        get guess
        count := count + 1
        if guess < hidden then
            put "You are low"
        elsif guess > hidden then
            put "You are high"
        else
            put "You got it in ", count, " guesses"
            exit
        end if
    end loop
end loop
```

Save the program on the disk as *number*.

Menus of Commands

Here is a summary of the various commands that are available in the Turing environment.

File		Edit		Search		Run	
New	⌘N	Undo	⌘Z	Find...	⌘F	Run	⌘R
Open...	⌘O			Find Next	⌘G	Set Arguments...	
Close	⌘W	Cut	⌘X	Find Next Error	⌘E		
		Copy	⌘C			Paragraph	
Save	⌘S	Paste	⌘V	Replace...	⌘L		
Save As...		Clear		Replace Same	⌘M		
Revert to Saved							
		Select All	⌘A				
Page Setup...		Show Clipboard					
Print...	⌘T						
Quit	⌘Q						

The **Quit** command is used when you are finished and want to return to the System desk top to **Eject** your disk.

Problems

1.   Clear the program window, then enter a short letter to your teacher telling her or him how exciting it is to be using the computer as a simple word processor. Print the letter if you have a printer. Store the letter on the disk under the file name *teacher*. Check the directory to see that it is there. The program window can be used to enter any kind of data.

2.   Change the letter you wrote for question 1 so that an extra paragraph is added about how simple it is to edit text on a computer. Arrange to send this same letter to a friend as well as to your teacher. Print both new letters if you have a printer. Store them as files called *teacher2* and *friend*. Check the directory to see that all three files are there.

3.   Here is a Turing program to type into the program window and run

```
% The "seesaw" program
% Makes saw tooth patterns
loop
    put "How many teeth do you want? (1–12) "
    var count: int
    get count
    put repeat ( " *          " , count)
    put repeat ( "   *      * " , count)
    put repeat ( "     *  *   " , count)
    put repeat ( "       *    " , count)
end loop
```

Try running the program. If you get tired of making saw tooth patterns you can stop the execution of the program by selecting **Stop** from the **Run** menu.

Editing The Program

- The **Edit** menu has a number of very useful commands for editing programs. If you want to delete parts of the text but do not want to use the backspace (delete) key you can select the text to be deleted by dragging the mouse over it. This will leave it highlighted. Now choose the **Cut** command from the **Edit** menu and the selected text will disappear.

- If you want the text to reappear, give the **Paste** command from the **Edit** menu.

- When text is cut it is stored on the **clipboard**.

- Selected text can be copied into the clipboard and not deleted (cut) from its present location by giving the **Copy** command from the **Edit** menu. Any **Cut** or **Copy** command will erase the previous contents of the clipboard and then place the currently selected text there.

- When the **Paste** command is given the clipboard's contents are inserted wherever the cursor is currently located. By moving the cursor you can paste text into any location you want.

- Pasting does not erase the clipboard, so you can paste the same text as many times as you like.

- Larger quantities of text can be selected more quickly than just by dragging the mouse over them. To select a whole line drag along the margin beside the line. You can select a passage of text by dragging diagonally from the beginning to the end.

- To select the entire text, use the **Select All** command from the **Edit** menu.

Problems

1.   Cutting and pasting is one way of editing in the program window. You cut or delete a line from one place in the text and paste or insert it into another. Try to cut a line of your text by dragging the mouse across it and then giving the **Cut** command from the **Edit** menu. Now move the cursor to the point in the text where you want to paste that line, and give the **Paste** command from the **Edit** menu. Give the command **Show Clipboard**. What happens?

2.   You can cut several lines by dragging from the beginning diagonally to the end. Now give the **Cut** command and see what happens. Then, use the **Paste** command. Now move the cursor between these two commands. Give the **Show Clipboard** command.

3.   You can copy text instead of deleting by using the **Copy** command. First select the portion of the text to be copied. Next use the **Copy**

command. Then, use the **Paste** command. Try this pair first without moving the cursor between commands. Then try it again, moving it between commands. Try a second **Paste** command without a **Copy** first. What do you get?

Note:

In the next section certain advanced features of the Turing editor are described; these can be referred to later.

Searching for and Replacing Text

To find the occurrence of a particular word in a text, choose the **Find...** command from the **Search** menu. When you do, a dialog box appears asking you to type in the text you are searching for. When you type this in the first occurrence of the sought for text following the cursor's current position is highlighted and the cursor moved to it. If you give the **Replace...** command from the **Search** menu you will get a dialog box that asks you what text you want to find and also what text you wanted to appear instead.

If you want to find the next occurrence of the same text select the **Find Next** command from the **Search** menu. You can replace this text using the **Replace** command, or leave it as it is. If you use the **Replace Same** command you do not need to use the **Find Next** command.

Redirecting Output to the Disk

Data that is output from a program can be stored as a disk file using the **Save as...** command with an active I/O window.

Another way to do this is to redirect the output that would normally go to the screen during execution, to go to a disk file. The picture shows a program called *counting*. When you use the command **Set Arguments...** from the **Run** menu, a dialog box appears.

To redirect the output from the screen to a disk file, click the mouse in the button opposite the word **File....** When you do, a second dialog box appears asking you to name the file where the output is to go. Here we entered the name *count*.

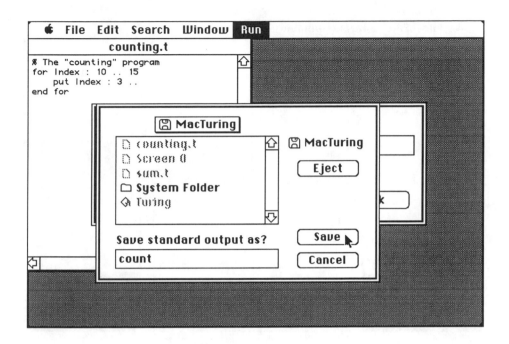

When the program is run, there is nothing in the I/O window; we did not enter any data during execution and we have redirected the output to the disk. To see that the output is on the disk, give the **Open...** command and select the *count* file from the directory. This will bring a third window onto the screen titled *count*. The window was hiding the program window when it first appeared so we dragged it down on the screen.

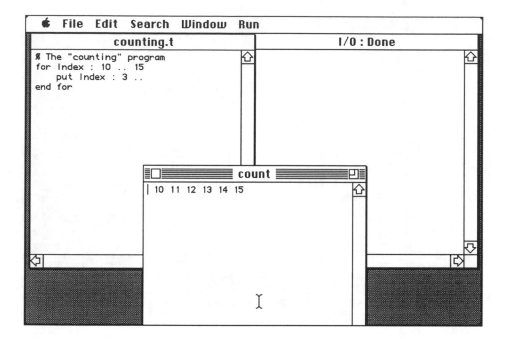

You can move an active window by putting the mouse pointer in its title bar and dragging it to a new position. To enlarge or shrink a window you putt the mouse pointer in the small box at its lower right corner (the size box) and drag. The corner moves in response.

Input Data from Disk Files

You can use a data file as input for a program. Here is a program that will read and output the numbers in the data file *count*

```
% The "echo" program
put "Enter five integers"
var number: int
for i: 1 .. 5
    get number
    put number
end for
```

This program expects five integers to be input. It will then echo these integers. First we will show what happens when the input is from the keyboard. Here is an example execution in which 10 is typed (shown in white) and then echoed (shown in black), then 11 is typed and echoed, and so on.

```
Enter five integers
10
10
11
11
12
12
13
13
14
14
15
15
```

Now suppose instead we use the **Set Arguments...** command and arrange that the input be redirected so it comes from the file called *count* rather than from the keyboard. Make sure that the output is going to the screen and not to a file. When you run, the I/O window will now look like this

```
Enter five integers
10
11
12
13
14
15
```

Since the input does not come from the keyboard, it does not appear in the I/O window. The result of the **put** statement shows you what was input. You can redirect both the input and the output by setting both input and output to files. Use a file named *list* for the output. Now nothing appears on the execution screen, but if you check the directory you can see that the file *list* is now there. Try opening it to see what it is like.

Technical Terms you should now know

toolbox

software

read-only memory (ROM)

application software

mouse

keyboard

menu bar

desk top

icon

program

data

Turing System

window

program window

I/O (or execution) window

error message window

dialog box

output from program

pointer

click

double click

press

drag

startup disk

disk icon

trash can

highlighting

command

selecting command

cursor

Eject command

Turing environment

text editor

active window

close box

character

backspace key (delete)

Return

File menu

New command

Print command

disk

disk drive

Save as... command

extension

directory of files on disk

scroll

Close command

Find Next Error command

Open... command

Run menu

Run command

Stop command
word processor
Edit menu
Cut command
Paste command
ShowClipboard command
Select All command
Search command
Replace... command

Find... command
Find Next command
data files on disk
size box
redirecting input from
    keyboard to disk
redirecting output from screen
    to disk

THE EDITOR FOR THE ICON

*In the editor we can enter
the program, correct any errors we
make in typing, and then run it*

In order to be able to enter a Turing program into the computer we need to use the **editor**.

In the editor we can enter the program, correct any errors we make in typing, and then run it.

To do this we make use of special **commands** that are not part of the Turing programming language. They are called **operating system** commands.

Some commands are given by typing single letters when the cursor is in the command position on the left margin of the program window. Longer commands are typed below the program window on the command line.

Still other commands are achieved by using special keys: the arrow key, the **Del** (delete) key, the **Ins** (insert) key, or the **ctrl** (control) key.

The Turing Environment

When you begin a session on an ICON computer it should be prepared to accept input from you. It should be in the **Turing Environment**. On the screen you will see a horizontal line near the bottom and a vertical line bordering the left-hand side. Near the top of the left border is a **line marker**.

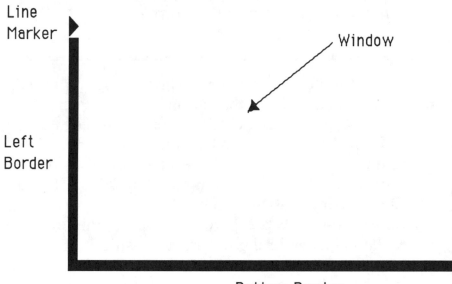

Line
Marker

Left
Border

Window

Bottom Border

These lines define a **window** into which you will be entering your Turing programs. It is called the **program window**.

Moving the Cursor

On the right-hand side of the keyboard you will see keys that are labelled with arrows. Press the one with the arrow pointing to the right and watch the screen. A blinking underline appears in the window just to the right of the line marker. This is the **cursor.** Press the right-arrow key again. The cursor moves over one space to the right on the same line. Now press the down-arrow key. The cursor moves down one line and the line marker follows it down one line on the left border. The line marker tells you what line the cursor is on. Now press the left-arrow key twice. The cursor moves over to the left border to the same position as the line marker.

Typing in the Window

Move the cursor so that it is near the middle of the screen then type "this is fun". Now see if you can type "THIS IS FUN" right below the first line. Move the cursor first to where you want to start typing, then either hold down a **shift key** (there is one on either the lower left or right side of the standard typewriter keys marked by a fat up-arrow) and type the **upper case** or **capital** letters.

When you are typing one line after another, it is convenient to use the **Enter** key, the one with the crooked left arrow just at the right of the standard typewriter keys. When you press Return, the cursor moves down one line and right over to the left side of the window. Notice how the line marker moves down so that it is always on the same line as the cursor.

You can get the cursor to move over to the left border by pressing the **Esc** (escape) key on the top left of the keyboard. If you type a letter when the cursor is in this position, you will have given the computer a **command**. Don't try this until you have learned what commands are possible.

Editing What You Have Typed

So far you see how to enter text into the window. One of the great things about computers is that you can change what you have entered very easily; you can **edit** the text.

The Turing Environment provides a simple word processor. You could use it, if you wanted to, for essays or letters. We will be using it mostly for writing Turing programs or preparing data for our programs.

- If you mistype a letter, or any **character** such as an asterisk, you can back up one space (by pressing the **backspace** key) and type the correct character. The original one is erased when you do this. You can also replace one character by another.

- To delete characters, move the cursor to the first character to be deleted, then press the **Del** (delete) key at the bottom of the numeric keypad for each character you want deleted.

- To insert characters, move the cursor to the character that is to follow the inserted characters and type the insertion. As you type, the characters on the same line following the insertion move over to make room. The insertion is terminated by pressing any one of the arrow keys or the escape key.

- Practice editing by changing your text from "this is fun" to "They say this is easy".

Erasing the Contents of the Input Window

If you want to get rid of everything in the window and start fresh you can do this by means of the **new** command.

- To give a command, you must first move the cursor to the command position which is on the left border of the window. The easiest way to do this is to press the Esc (escape) key. When you are in the command position on the left border and want to give a command that requires more than one letter, type a colon (:). When you do this, a colon appears below the window in what we call the **command line**.

- Type the command word *new* followed by Return. You will be asked to verify that you meant to start a new session. Type a *y* (for yes) and then Return. As soon as you do this the window will be cleared and the line marker will be located at the top line.

- When you finish using the computer, you should type the *new* command so the next user can begin with a fresh clean window.

Printing What You Have Typed

If you have a printer attached to your computer, you can get a printed version of what you typed in the program window. To do this, move the cursor to the left border, type a colon and then type *print* followed by Return. The word *print* is a command which can be used to produce a **hard copy** of your input.

Saving What You Have Typed on the Disk

Often we want to save what we have typed on the screen more permanently and in a form that can be read by the computer. To do this we must store it. Normally on the ICON you store things on the hard drive of the file server, but it is possible to store on a floppy disk. What you store on the disk remains there even if the computer is shut off and the disk removed from the drive. In order to use the disk memory, you must have a disk that has been prepared to work in the Turing Environment. It has to be **formatted** so that information such as programs and data can be stored on it. We will assume that your instructor has given you a formatted.

• When you have typed something in the window that you would like to save on the disk, place the disk in the disk drive . The label side of the disk should be up, with the exposed slot on the disk towards the computer. Shut the door of the disk drive.

• You must now give the command that states the name of the file that the information you have typed is to have on the disk and request that it be written there. Suppose we have a letter in the window which has a first line

Dear Mr. Dale:

You must choose a name for the file on the disk to contain the letter, say *Dale*. Then we would give the *w* (for write) command

:w Dale

in order to write this letter on to the disk under the file name *Dale*.

• When you give the write command the disk will make a whirring sound and the letter will be recorded on it.

Your Computer Disk

Be careful how you handle your disk. Keep it protected when not in use. When you put it into the disk drive do not force it into the slot. Keep it clean and dry and never touch the exposed part.

Listing a Directory of Files on the Disk

To check that the letter is on the disk you can look at the **directory** of files. To do this type the command

:dir

This command will list the names of files, such as *Dale*, that have been stored on the disk. All files are listed in the directory using capital letters even though you can refer to them by little letters or a mixture of capital and little letters.

Deleting a File from the Disk

To delete the *Dale* file from the disk you give the command

:delete Dale

Try doing this and then give the

:dir

command to see that it has vanished. If you still have the *Dale* letter in the window you can write it again to the disk by the command

:w Dale

Renaming a File on the Disk

To change the name of a disk file use the command

:rename old-name new-name

Try changing the name of the *Dale* letter to *teacher*. Look at the directory to see if you did this. Names of files should be limited to 8 characters optionally followed by a period with three characters more after the period. These last three characters are called the **extension**. Remember, for file names it does not matter whether you use upper or lower case letters.

Editing a File

To edit a file that is on the disk use the command

:e file-name

This will clear the window and bring the file you name into the window. You can see the name of the file in the window by giving the single letter f (for file) command. The name of the file currently in the window (if it has a name) is displayed below the window.

* If you want to rename the file in the window, you can do it by giving the command

:f new-name

* To write a file in the window onto disk using its current name, you need only give the single letter command w (for write). No two files on disk may have the same name so that, if you write a file with a certain name that is the same as the name of a file on disk, the file on disk is erased and the new version written over it. You must be careful in writing a file on disk that you do not destroy one that you wanted. When you bring a new file into the window it erases what is already there; so be careful. You can not damage the computer but you can erase your own files.

- If you have two disk drives, each drive can have a file with a given name and copying from one disk to another is possible.

Saving Turing Programs on the Disk

Turing programs are typed, edited, and stored on disk just as any other text is. Here is a program for you to type in and store on the disk.

```
% The "times" program
% Outputs a multiplication table
var number: int
put "Choose a number between 1 and 12 " ..
get number
put "Here is the multiplication table for ",number
for i: 1 .. 12
    put i: 2, " times ", number, " is ", i*number: 2
end for
```

Store the program as a file called *times*. After you store it give the **Run** command. To give the **Run** command, press the escape key, then give the command *r* (for run). You can also give the **Run** command by pressing the **function key** F1 which is at the upper left corner of the keyboard. When the prompting line

Choose a number between 1 and 12 _

appears on the screen, the cursor is sitting after the 12. You should then type a number between 1 and 12 inclusive. When you finish typing press Return or the computer will not know you have finished. As soon as you do, the multiplication table will appear for the number you have chosen.

Here is a sample output screen:

```
     Choose a number between 1 and 12 6
     Here is the multiplication table for 6

          1 times 6 is   6
          2 times 6 is  12
          3 times 6 is  18
          4 times 6 is  24
          5 times 6 is  30
          6 times 6 is  36
          7 times 6 is  42
          8 times 6 is  48
          9 times 6 is  56
         10 times 6 is  60
         11 times 6 is  66
         12 times 6 is  72
```

Suppose you wanted to have a table showing your number multiplied by the values 1 to 20 rather than 1 to 12. What change in the program might do this? Try changing it then run it again. Store the changed program under a new name, say *times20*.

Try changing the program by substituting a / for the * in the program. You will have a division table instead of a multiplication table. Can you fix the rest of the program to suit this change? Store this program as *divide* on the disk.

Here is a slightly longer program. It is stored on the disk of program examples from this book. You can bring it into the window by giving the command

:e number

(If you do not have it on your disk you can type it in yourself.)

When it is in the window give the run command and play the guessing game. After you have played the game try reading the program to see if you can understand some of it even before you have learned anything about the Turing language.

Here is the program:

```
% The "number" program
% Chooses a number at random between 1 and 99
% and allows you to guess it
var hidden, guess: int
var reply: string(1)
put "See if you can guess the hidden number"
put "It is between 1 and 99 inclusive"
loop
    var count: int := 0
    put "Do you want to play? Answer y or n " ..
    get reply
    exit when reply = "n"
    % Choose a random number between 1 and 99
    randint (hidden, 1, 99)
    loop
        put "Enter your guess ",
            "(any number between 1 and 99) " ..
        get guess
        count := count + 1
        if guess < hidden then
            put "You are low"
        elsif guess > hidden then
            put "You are high"
        else
            put "You got it in ", count, " guesses"
            exit
        end if
    end loop
end loop
```

Problems

1.   Clear the screen, then enter a short letter to your teacher telling her or him how exciting it is to be using the computer as a simple word processor. Print the letter if you have a printer. Store the letter on the disk under the file name *teacher*. Check the directory to see that it is there.

2.   Change the letter you wrote for question 1 so that an extra paragraph is added about how simple it is to edit text on a computer. Arrange to send this same letter to a friend as well as to your teacher. Print both new letters if you have a printer. Store them as files called *teacher2* and *friend*. Check the directory to see that all three files are there.

Editing Lines Rather than Characters

- You can delete whole lines by moving the cursor to the left border, opposite the line to be deleted, and then giving the command *d*   for delete.

- To insert a line, move the cursor in the left border to point to the line to follow the insertion and type *i* to insert. The line you were pointing to moves down to make room for an inserted line and the cursor is in the window so you can begin typing the new line. When you have finished, go back to the left border by pressing the Esc key.

- If you want to add a new line after the line you are currently pointing at, use the command *a* for append.

- You can also insert or append a number of lines. Pressing Return after each line moves the cursor down so you can start typing the next line.

Substituting One String of Characters for Another

If we wanted to change one word into another we could do it by deleting the original word and inserting the replacement. This can also be done by using the **substitute** command. The **substitute** command allows you to change a string in the current line, called the **source string** to another string, called the **target string** As with the other commands of more than one letter like *new* or *print*, we first type the special signal colon (:). Now type in the substitute command. For example, to change the word *good* into the word *great* you would type

> :s/good/great/

The *s* is for substitute. The source string is *good* and the target string is *great* . If the line used to say "Have a good day", it now says "Have a great day".

Problems

1.   Experiment with what happens when you put the cursor on the left border opposite a line of typing and give the command *d*. What happens when you follow this immediately by the command *u* ? (The *d* stands for delete; the *u* stands for undelete.)

2.   Experiment with the command *a* (for append) which allows you to append lines after the line you are pointing at when you give this append command.

3.   Experiment with the command *i* (for insert) which allows you to insert lines preceding the line you are currently pointing at when you give this insert command. What is the difference between insert and append?

4.   Cutting and pasting is one way of editing in a word processor. You cut or delete a line from one place in the text and paste or insert it into another. Try to cut a line of your text using the *d* command, then, by moving the line marker to the line following where you want to paste that line, undelete the line with a *u* command.

5.   You can cut several lines by marking the lines. You mark lines by placing the line marker at the first line to be cut, giving the *m* (for mark) command, then moving the line marker down using the down arrow to the last line to be marked. Now give the *d* command and see what happens. Next, use the *u* command. Now move the line marker between the *d* and the *u* commands, after you mark the lines.

6.   You can copy text, instead of deleting it, by using the *t* (for take) command on the line to be copied then the *u* command on the line to follow the copy. Try this pair first without moving the line marker between commands then move it between commands. You copy several lines by first marking the lines with the *m* command then using the *t* and *u* commands. Try doing this.

7.   Here is a Turing program to type into the window and run

```
% The "seesaw" program
% Makes saw tooth patterns
loop
    put "How many teeth do you want? (1–12) "
    var count: int
    get count
    put repeat ("*          " , count)
    put repeat ("  *      *" , count)
    put repeat ("    *  *  " , count)
    put repeat ("      *    " , count)
end loop
```

Try running the program. If you get tired of making saw tooth patterns you can stop the execution of the program by pressing certain keys on the keyboard. Ask your teacher which keys provide the control-break feature on your machine.

Note:

The next two sections describe advanced features of the editor; they can be referred to later.

Redirecting Output to a Disk File

If you want to save the output of a program on a disk file you can give a run command in this form:

:r > filename

The output will not appear on the screen but will be in the disk file named.

This will allow you to print output by bringing the file containing the data into the program window and giving the command

:print

You can redirect the output to the printer (without saving it on disk) by giving the command

:r > printer

Input Data from a Disk File

Instead of having input data come from the keyboard you can have it come from a disk file. Suppose you have stored the data in a file called *data*. You can run the program with this as input data by giving the command

:r < data

You must remember that the data read in from the file (instead of the keyboard) will not appear echoed in the execution window as data from the keyboard. If you want to see it, you would have to include an extra output instruction after every input instruction.

Technical Terms you should now know

Turing Environment
line marker
window
output from program
keyboard
arrow keys
cursor
shift key
Num Lock key
numeric keyboard
command
escape key
text editor
word processor
character
delete key
insert key
space bar
command line
Return
erase command (:new)
print command (:print)
diskette

formatted diskette
floppy disk
disk drive
w (for write) command
extension
directory of files on disk
:dir (for directory) command
deleting a disk file (*:delete*)
renaming a disk file (*:rename*)
editing a file (*:e*)
f (for file) command
r (for run) command
F1 (run) command
control-c (to stop execution) on
　　　some systems ctrl-b
line editor
d (for delete or cut) command
s (for substitute) command
m (for mark) command
t (for take or copy) command
redirecting output
redirecting input

Chapter 3

PROBLEMS THAT YOU KNOW HOW TO SOLVE

*. . . a good memory
is one of the most powerful
assets we can have.*

To begin the study of problem solving and computer programming we will examine problems that are not really problems because we know the answers.

Memory saves us the trouble of solving the problem.

As we go along we will be building a repertoire of problems that we know how to solve and a good memory is one of the most powerful assets we can have.

Even so, we must learn how to actually solve problems for which we do not know the answer, perhaps because we can not remember the answer or because we never did know it.

When we want to have the assistance of a computer to get the answers to problems we find there is a second problem: How to instruct the computer to do our work for us.

We must learn a language in which the instructions can be given and we must learn to express our own know-how so that the computer too will know how.

The computer does not solve problems. But you can use it to help you solve a problem.

Questions and Answers about Arithmetic Problems

Q.   When is a problem not a problem?
A.   When you already know the answer.

Q.   What is 2 and 2?
A.   4.

Q.   How do you know the answer?
A.   Because I solved the problem before and remember the answer.

Q.   Do you remember how you solved it before?
A.   I'm not sure. Maybe by putting out two stones and another two stones and counting them to see that there were four stones altogether.

Q.   Would the same result have occurred if you had used apples instead of stones?
A.   Of course, that's how I know two and two make four. I generalized the result.

Q.   How do you express this abstract idea in a mathematical notation?
A.   By writing $2 + 2 = 4$. This is a part of my memory bank of arithmetic results – number facts as I used to call them.

Q.   Do you remember all the number facts you ever learned?
A.   I sometimes forget the multiplication table, like what are six nines. But I have a hand calculator that gives me the answer quickly.

Q.   How do you know how to get the answer on the hand calculator?
A.   That's not a problem. I remember how: You push "clear", then the "6", then the "×", then "9", then the "equals", and the answer appears "54".

Q.   What happens if you reverse the order of pushing the "9" and the "6"?
A.   I'd get the same result.

Q.   How do you know?

A.   I remember that the order of the two numbers in a multiplication operation doesn't matter.

Q.   How do you state that as an abstract generalization?

A.   Multiplication is commutative. (Aren't you impressed?)

Q.   Can you prove it?

A.   No, but I can try a whole lot of cases, for example, $5 \times 8 = 40$ and $8 \times 5 = 40$. (I just tested it on my calculator.)

Q.   O.K. What is $(2 + 3) \times 5$?

A.   25; I should say $(2 + 3) \times 5 = 25$.

Q.   Is it the same as $2 + 3 \times 5$?

A.   No that would be 17. In the first example I added 2 and 3, because they were in brackets, then multiplied the result by 5. In the second, since multiplication comes before addition, I multiplied 3 by 5 to get 15, then added the 2 to get the final result 17.

Q.   Can you state a rule for remembering the sequence in which arithmetic operations are done?

A.   Sure BEDMAS; first Brackets, then Exponentiation, then Division, then Multiplication, then Addition, and finally Subtraction.

Q.   What is Exponentiation?

A.   Things like 3 squared and 6 cubed. You write them with exponents: 3^2 and 6^3.

Q.   What is 3^2 equal to?

A.   9; the same as 3×3. And $6^3 = 6 \times 6 \times 6 = 216$.

Q.   Do you know the name for these rules for sequencing arithmetic operations?

A.   Rule of precedence?

Q.   Is that a question?

A.   I thought that is what my math teacher taught me.

Q.   Actually division and multiplication have the same precedence which
      is higher than that of addition and subtraction which have the same
      precedence.

A.   I know.

Q.   You know how to do arithmetic calculations on your hand calculator.
      Can you do them on a computer?

A.   That's a problem.

Q.   If I showed you how, would it still be a problem?

A.   No, I'd know then (if I could remember).

Basic Facts about Computer Programming

Let's start with a few facts about computers. (The special technical terms
will be in **boldface** type.)

- Computers can do things for you if you give them the **instructions** for
  doing them.

- A sequence of instructions for a computer is called a **computer
  program**. These instructions are sometimes called **statements.**

- Programs are written in a **programming language** just as number facts
  can be written in a mathematical language.

- We will be using the **Turing programming language** because it is very
  easy to learn and yet very powerful. Other languages that beginners use
  for programming include Basic and Pascal. Turing is much like Pascal
  but easier to use.

- Turing programs are easy for *you* to understand which is one of the most
  important properties of a good programming language.

- Turing programs can be "understood" by a huge variety of computers:
  microcomputers like PCs and Macs, as well as bigger computers.

- The computer must have the **Turing System Software** stored in its **memory** to run (execute) a Turing program.

- The system software let's you **enter** and **edit** your program, then let's you **run** it.

- When the computer runs your program, it first **translates** or **compiles** your program into a language that the computer can interpret, and then executes this translated program.

The First Program

Now we are ready to have the computer solve arithmetic problems. Here is the Turing program to add 2 and 2:

put 2 + 2

It consists of one instruction. The **keyword put** means to output on the **screen** of the computer. The 2 + 2 is an **output item**. The result of running this single-instruction program is that 4 is output on the screen.

The 2 + 2 is an **arithmetic expression**. Arithmetic expressions are made up of numbers and **arithmetic operators**. The arithmetic operators for Turing are the normal mathematical ones with two exceptions: multiplication is written as * instead of x and exponentiation is written using ** (3^2 is written as 3**2).

Here they are:

B	( )
E	* *
D	/
M	*
A	+
S	−

Now you can get the machine to produce the answers for many arithmetic problems that you already know how to solve. Here is the program to compute the value of $(2 + 3) \times 5$:

put $(2 + 3) * 5$

Problems

What is the Turing program to compute:

1. 2 multiplied by 3
2. $2 + 3 \times 5$
3. $(2 + 13) / 5$
4. $2 \times (6 + 3) / 4$
5. 2^5

Run each program then save it on your disk. Use disk file names like *arith1, arith2,* and so on.

Labelling Your Computer Results

When you write a program like

put $2 + 2$

The result 4 is displayed on the screen. You really should get the computer to display a more complete result, namely

$2 + 2 = 4$

To do this, we modify the program so that the output (**put**) instruction has two output items which you separate by a comma.

put "2 + 2 = ", $2 + 2$

The second output item is the same as before. The first output item is a **string** of characters surrounded by quotation marks. We call this a **string constant**. Now the display produced by running the program is

```
2 + 2 = 4
```

The second output item produced the 4, the first output item, namely "2 + 2 = ", is just copied but with the quotation marks removed.

Errors that you might make

- Confusing the meaning of the output items "2 + 2" and 2 + 2.

- Forgetting to have a matched pair of parentheses: writing
    put (2 + 3 * 5.

- Forgetting and writing an x instead of * for multiplication.

- Forgetting what you use as the operator for exponentiation.

- Forgetting to save a program.

- Using the same name for a changed program as the one on the disk when you wanted to keep both the original and the changed program.

Problems

1.   Edit the programs you created for the arithmetic problems earlier in this chapter so that the output is properly labelled in each one. Bring each program from the disk into the program window, edit it, run it, then save it back on the disk under the same name.

2.   Write programs to evaluate these arithmetic expressions. Check your computer results using a calculator.

  a. $7 + 6 \times 3 / 2$
  b. $(5 - 3) \times 3$
  c. $(7 - 12) / (6 - 1)$
  d. $(52 - 4) / 3$
  e. $5 / 2 + 1 / 2$
  f. $7 / 3 - 1$

How is the result output for part f different from the other parts?

Questions for Discussion

1.   Is division commutative? Show an example to explain your answer.

2.   Is subtraction commutative? Show an example to explain.

3.   A multiplication table is to be written with 10 rows numbered from 1 to 10, and 10 columns numbered from 1 to 10. Can you create it all simply by addition without having to remember any of the "times" table?

4.   If you were creating the table of question 3, how many of the 100 entries would you have to work out before you could just copy results previously obtained? Hint: remember 8×5 is the same as 5×8.

5.   When you have two numbers separated by an arithmetic operator such as 2 + 3 it can be called a binary operation. Simple binary arithmetic operations like adding two numbers are easy on a hand calculator. Why is

the evaluation of more complicated arithmetic expressions like 2 / 3 + 7 * 25 more difficult?

6.   Would a person using a hand calculator be able to evaluate a complicated arithmetic expression in less time than a person would by creating and running a Turing program to get the same result? Try it with a friend on some complicated expressions to see who wins.

7.   All the examples of arithmetic expressions in this chapter involve integers (whole numbers). Are the results always integers? What do we call a number that is not an integer?

8.   What result would you expect to get if the calculation produced a very large integer such as this program

put 5**12

Try it.

9.   Why do we say that the mathematical statement.

2 + 2 = 4

is an abstraction?

Technical Terms you should now know

generalization

abstraction

mathematical notation

arithmetic operator

commutative operation

precedence of arithmetic
    operations

exponentiation

instruction

statement

program

programming language

Turing programming language

Basic

Pascal

microcomputer

run

execute

Turing System Software

memory

translation

compiling

screen

output

keyword

put

output item

string

string constant

disk file

binary operation

operand

Chapter 4

GENERALIZATION

We discover how to solve
general problems by observing
particular instances.

In the last chapter we saw how to get the computer to add 2 and 2 to produce the result 4.

We did a lot more than that. We evaluated more complex arithmetic expressions involving integers.

The computer could be programmed to do what any hand calculator can do.

In this chapter we will see how to instruct the computer to add any two integers that we give it and produce their sum. This will be a more **general** program than the one for adding 2 and 2.

We will then see how to produce programs of this type that are more useful. We will solve this more general problem by **analogy** with the particular problem of adding 2 and 2.

We discover how to solve general problems by observing particular instances.

Questions and Answers about General Programs

Q.   In a computer program that will add any two integers how would you refer to the integers?

A.   I guess you would have to give them names.

Q.   What would you call them?

A.   I'd have to make up names, like *A* and *B*.

Q.   Then what will be the output instruction in the program to produce their sum?

A.   **put** A + B

Q.   Great. You solved the problem by analogy with the 2 + 2 problem. How does the computer know the values for *A* and *B* ?

A.   It would have to input the values.

Q   How can you enter values?

A.   By typing them in on the keyboard.

Q.   How would you instruct the computer to read them?

A.   By having an input instruction in the program. (I guessed that by analogy with the output instruction.)

Q.   If I tell you that the keyword in the input instruction corresponding to the keyword **put** in the output instruction is **get**, what would you expect the input instruction that reads the value for *A* to be?

A.   **get** A

Q.   And for *B* ?

A.   **get** B

Q.   So what is the program?

A.   **get** A

              get B

              put A + B

Q.   Where do you suppose the computer stores the values you enter for *A*
       and *B* before it outputs their sum?

A.   In its memory?

Q.   Sure. But when you intend to use its memory to hold a value you
       have to tell it to reserve space for that value. How do you do that?

A.   I don't know. Tell me.

Storing Values in the Computer's Memory

- To reserve space in the memory of the computer, you must give it a list
  of names of the values you will be using and tell it what type of values
  they are.

- So far we have had only one type of value, namely numbers that are
  integers.

- To make a reservation to store a value named *A* that is an integer we
  write in the program

              var A: **int**

- Both **var** and **int** are Turing keywords. The **int** means that any value we
  store in memory location called *A* will have to be an integer. The
  keyword **var** is short for **variable** This is because the values that we will
  store in memory location *A* will vary.

- Notice that there is a colon between the name of the variable and its type.

- We call these program statements, that start with the keyword **var**,
  variable declarations. A variable declaration in the program must
  precede any instruction that refers to the variable.

- If we want to declare several variables of the same type (integer, for example), we can write a single declaration

  var A, B: **int**

  The variable names in the list are separated by commas and ended by a colon.

- In the same way we can use a single input instruction to input values into *A* and *B* using

  get A, B

- So the complete program for adding any two values can be

  var A, B: **int**
  get A, B
  put A + B

- This is a slightly longer program. Any program that uses the memory to store values must have at least one variable declaration.

- Now you can run the program. You must enter the two integers you want to add. These must be separated from each other by at least one blank or a return (enter). This is called **white space**.

- Here is a sample **execution window**:

```
5 32
37
```

We have shown the two numbers that you enter in bold face. What the computer outputs is shown in regular. On the computer screen they are both displayed the same way. When 5 was entered, it was placed in the variable called A and 32 was placed in the variable called B as shown here.

Here is another execution window, obtained on another run of the program:

```
2
18
20
```

The first integer you enter will be stored in memory location A. It will become the value of variable A. The second will be the value of variable B. In the first example, the two numbers entered are separated by a blank; in the second by a return. You must always have a return after you are finished entering the two numbers or else the **get** instruction cannot execute.

• If you want to see for yourself what the value of a variable is, you can ask for its value to be output. To see A, include the instruction

   put A

To see B, include the instruction

   put B

- If you try to output the value of a variable before any value has been stored there, you will get an **error message** telling you that the variable is **uninitialized**. This means it has not yet been given any value.

- If we include this instruction

  put A, B

  in our program just before the

  put A + B

  instruction, this is a sample execution window:

```
6
55
655
71
```

In the first two lines the values that we entered on the keyboard are **echoed** on the screen as we type each item, the first value 6 being stored in A, the second 55 being stored in B. The last two lines come from the two **put** statements in the program. The last is the sum of A and B. The second last contains the values of A then B. Notice that, on output, values are run together with no space between them. We will see how to create spaces between output items later.

Labelling Input and Output

When you run the program we have produced, the result will be a blank execution window until you type the values for *A* and *B*, then the results will appear. It is not a good idea to leave the user of a program wondering what to do. You should **prompt** the user (even yourself) by outputting a **message** by an instruction such as

> **put** "Enter two integers, separated by spaces or return"

Also you should, as before, label the output with this output instruction

> **put** A, " + ", B, " = ", A + B

instead of simply

> **put** A + B

with these changes the program might be:

> **var** A, B: **int**
> **put** "Enter two integers, separated by spaces or return"
> **get** A, B
> **put** "A = ", A, " B = ", B
> **put** A, " + ", B, " = ", A + B

Here now is a sample execution window:

```
Enter two integers, separated by spaces or return
12  32
A = 12 B = 32
12 + 32 = 44
```

The third instruction in the program is not really necessary, but we have included it to show how you might display the values assigned to A and B also with labels. To prevent them running together, we included a space inside the quotation marks around the = signs and before B = .

Problems

The problems marked with an asterisk are more mathematical.

Write programs that have input prompts and output labels that:

1.   Compute the cube of any integer that you input.

2.   Compute the result of dividing two integers. Notice the number of digits output in the answers in different cases.

3.   Instead of using the division operator / use the division operator **div** and investigate the results by replacing the output instruction in the example by this instruction.

    put A **div** B

*4.   Compute the square of the hypotenuse of a right-angled triangle given the other two sides as integers.

*5.   Change the program of question 4 to compute the length of the hypotenuse. Note: The result of this program is to produce the output 2

    put sqrt(4)

The **function** *sqrt* produces the square root of the value that follows in parentheses.

Real Numbers

- So far we have just been using integers in our calculations. The input data was of the type **int**. The other **data type** for numbers is **real**

- Any number with a decimal point is a **real number**. Sometimes it is a **fraction** expressed as a decimal fraction like .25. Sometimes it is a **mixed number** like 5.7 with an **integer part** and a **fraction part**.

- Even an integer like 5 can be written with a decimal point as 5. although we do not usually do this. We say that integers are, in fact, real numbers; but not all real numbers are integers.

- Whenever a variable is to contain a real number that is not an integer, it must be declared as **real**.

- In the memory a real number is stored as two parts, one part giving the sequence of digits of the real number, the **significant digits**, the other part giving the position of the decimal point among the digits. This latter part is sometimes referred to as the **exponent part** because it represents the power of 10 that must multiply the significant digits part if it is treated as an integer. For example, 5.75 can be written as

$$575 \times 10^{-2}$$

The significant digits would be 575. The exponent would be −2.

- In Turing, whenever real numbers can be output as integers or mixed numbers, with the decimal point in its proper position, they will be. If too many significant digits have to be displayed as would be the case with very large or very small numbers, the real number is output in the **exponent form**. For example,

.0000000032

would be shown as

3.2e − 9

- Here is a program to output the area of a circle when you input the radius:

```
var radius: real
put "Enter radius of circle in cm."
get radius
put "Area of circle of radius = ", radius, " cm. is ",
        3.14159 * radius ** 2,  " sq.cm."
```

Notice how the blanks included in the string constants keep the output properly spaced.

Assignment Statements and Constants

- You can also use an **assignment statement** to give a value to a variable. For example, if you have declared a real variable called *area* with this declaration:

```
var area: real
```

then you can assign the value 4.37 to *area* by having this instruction

```
area := 4.37
```

- The left-hand side of the assignment must be the name of a variable. On the right-hand side of the := is the value to be assigned to the variable. This value must be of the same data type as the variable, just as values input must have the same data type as the variables in which they are to be stored.

- We think of the := as a left pointing arrow, which tells the computer to move the value 4.37 into the variable named *area*, as shown here.

area

- Some variables in programs are assigned a value and that value never changes in the program; its value is constant. We can use a special type of "variable" called a **constant**. In declaring a constant, the value to be assigned to it appears in the declaration. In our circle program we could define a constant called *pi* by this declaration

  const pi: **real** := 3.14159

  then in the expression for the *area* we could use *pi* instead of having an unexplained mystery number 3.14159 appear there. In declaring constants, we can leave out the data type since the value assigned to it tells the type. We can write instead:

  const pi := 3.14159

- So our circle program might now be written as:

  ```
  const pi := 3.14159
  var radius, area: real
  put "Enter radius of circle in cm."
  get radius
  area := pi * radius ** 2
  put "Area of circle of radius = ", radius, " cm. is ",
          area, " sq.cm."
  ```

  This program does exactly what the previous program did but it is easier to understand. We want our programs to be as easy to understand as possible.

Division of Integers

Whenever two integers are divided, the result of the division is a real number. That number may just happen also to be an integer but, if the value is to be assigned to a variable, the variable must be declared as **real** For example, this program:

> **var** answer: **int**
> answer := 6 / 3

will produce an error message. If you want to produce an integer result from a division process, you can choose one of two alternatives. One uses the **div** operator

> answer := 6 **div** 3

and the other uses the Turing function *round*

> answer := round (6 / 3)

In the first case, the answer is the integer that comes from dividing and chopping off any fractional part of the result. In the second, the result is rounded to the nearest integer. In this example, both methods produce exactly the same answer, namely 2, since the answer is 2.0000. If the integers to be divided are 11 and 3, the result of 11 **div** 3 is 3, and the result of *round* (11 / 3) is 4, since the result of 11 / 3 is 3.6666667.

Often you want to know the **remainder** when two integers are divided using the **div** operator. This is obtained using the **mod** operator

> 11 **mod** 3

This **mod** operator will produce a 2, the remainder when 11 is divided by 3.

The **mod** operator is commonly used to test whether an integer is even or odd. If a value is stored in the integer variable *number* , then

> number **mod** 2

will have a zero value if *number* is even, and a value 1 if *number* isodd.

Understandable Programs and Comments

Programs that are not easy to understand are bad programs even though they give correct answers. Frequently, programs must be modified at a later date. If the person who is to modify them cannot understand them, then he or she must start over and waste all the original programmer's effort . Sometimes we say they have to "reinvent the wheel." There are a number of ways of making your programs more understandable:

- Use a good programming language. Turing is such a language.

- Choose names for variables that describe what the values they store represent. For example, choose the name *radius* to store the radius of a circle. Names of variables must begin with a letter and consist of letters and digits. They must not contain any special characters like + or / or a blank. You can use upper or lower case letters.

- Prompt input and label output so that the program is **user friendly**.

- In addition you can add **comments** in English to your program whenever the Turing instructions seem to require a little explanation. These comments are inserted anywhere in a program between statements and instructions but not in the middle of instructions. Comments are sometimes referred to as program **documentation**.

- A comment must begin with the symbol % and end with a return. For example, this comment might be used to start the program that calculates the area of a circle:

% Compute the area of a circle given its radius

- You should make a habit of having a comment that explains the purpose of a program right at the beginning.

- A second very useful comment is one that gives the file name of the program on the disk. For example, as the first line of the circle program we could write

% The "circle" program

and store the program on disk under the name *circle*. We can then use the file name to refer to the program when we want to say something about it.

Errors that you might make

- Typing the wrong character, the letter 'O' for a digit zero or the letter 'l' for a digit one.

- Forgetting to declare a variable.

- Choosing a variable name that has a blank or a special character in it, like *six+seven*.

- Choosing a variable name that starts with a digit, like *3rdpage*.

- Misspelling a variable name: declaring it as *topMark* and using the name *topmark* in an assignment. Turing is case sensitive. It treats the capital letter 'M' as different from the uncapped letter 'm'.

- Forgetting the colon in an assignment statement: writing sum = sum + 1.

- Entering data of the wrong type: say a string value instead of an integer.

- Splitting a line in the middle of a string constant.

- Splitting a line in the middle of a comment.

- Forgetting to press Return after data has been entered.

- Trying to assign the result of a division of integers to an integer variable.

- Using a reserved word in Turing as a variable name.

All these errors are errors in the use of the programming language, what we call **syntax errors**, and will be discovered by the computer. When a syntax error is discovered, an error message is displayed on the screen. Getting rid of errors in a program is called **debugging**.

Most of these errors are discovered at the time of program translation and are called **compile-time** errors. Others, such as trying to enter a string instead an integer, are discovered at the time of program execution and are called **run-time** errors.

The error messages you get are sometimes hard to understand, but by looking at the program you can usually see what is wrong. Read the messages carefully.

Sometimes a single error will cause a series of error messages. You should try to correct it and run again. It is usually worth while to look at each error message in a series and see if you have made a series of mistakes.

Problems

The problems marked with an asterisk are more mathematical.

Write programs to carry out the calculations required in each problem. In these programs be sure to choose good variable names and include the comments that give the program's disk file name and explain what it is to do. Remember to have input prompts and output labels.

1.   Compute the weight of a person in kilograms given the weight in pounds.

2.   Compute the age of a person given their year of birth and the present year.

3.   Compute the new balance in a bank account given the initial balance and the amount deposited.

4.   Compute the tax on an item purchased and the total to be paid given the cost of the item and the fact that there is a 15% sales tax.

5.   Compute the cost of an item given the amount paid for it including a 15% sales tax.

6.   Compute the average speed of a trip (in km per hour) given the starting time and the finishing time (in hours and minutes), and the trip distance in kilometers.

*7.   Compute the volume of a cylinder given its height and the radius of the base in centimeters.

*8.   Compute the volume of a sphere given its radius in centimeters.

*9.   Compute the temperature in Celsius given the temperature in Fahrenheit. Note: A Fahrenheit degree is 5 / 9 of a Celsius degree and 0°C is 32°F.

Questions for Discussion

1.   Why do most people understand particular examples more easily than general statements?

2.   Why do we bother with general statements at all?

3.   Why is it important that we prompt input and label output?

4.   Why do we bother with integer variables when all numerical calculations could be done with real numbers?

5.   Turing is a language that does not require you to put any special signal, such as a semicolon, at the end of each statement. Could you type a Turing program all on one line?

Technical Terms you should now know

analogy
keyboard
input instruction
get
variable
declaration of variable
var
white space
return
enter
execution window
initialization
initialized variable
echo of input
prompt
message
sqrt
div
mod

real number
data type
fraction
mixed number
integer part
fraction part
significant digits
exponent
exponent form of real number
assignment statement
constant
comment
documentation
user friendly program
disk file name
syntax error
debugging
compile-time error
run-time error

Chapter 5

BASIC DATA TYPES:
INTEGER, REAL, AND STRING

All data in a computer is
represented as a series of bits . . .

Information in a computer is stored in **binary form** –
the scale of two.

Our usual way of representing numbers is in **decimal
form** – the scale of ten.

In binary form, there are only two digits 0 and 1. In
decimal form there are ten digits: 0, 1, 2, 3, 4, 5, 6, 7, 8,
9.

Either one of these forms is a digital form, and the
computers are called **digital computers**.computers,
digital

Each binary digit is called a **bit**. All the data in a
computer is represented as a series of bits, but the
different types of data require a different number of bits.

That is why we must declare the type of data that is to
be stored in the memory: so a sufficient number of bits is
reserved for it.

We have looked at the integer and real data types in
the last chapter. Here we will concentrate on the string
type.

Questions and Answers about Data Types

Q.   Why do computers use binary representation of information?

A.   Because there are many physical devices that have two states. For example, a light switch can be on or off.

Q.   What has that got to do with the binary form?

A.   In binary form there are only two digits which we usually call 0 and 1 because we are used to these two digits from the decimal system.

Q.   Can you count in the binary system?

A.   Of course, I do it by analogy with the decimal system.

Q.   What happens when you have 2 objects? How would you write this in binary form?

A.   I guess it would be the same way as if I had ten objects in the decimal system?

Q.   For ten in the decimal system you put a 1 in the tens position and start over in the units position with zero. The number two in binary corresponds to ten in the decimal system. So what is two in binary form?

A.   It should be 10.

Q   Right. What is three in binary?

A.   It should be 11. And four would be 100. That looks like one hundred.

Q.   You know it is not one hundred because you are working in the binary system. Each binary digit is called a bit. How many bits does it take to represent one decimal digit – any decimal digit?

A.   The biggest decimal digit is 9. And nine in binary would be 1001, if I am right. So it takes four bits to represent a decimal digit.

Q.   Right.

Representation of Data Types

There are three basic data types that we will use a great deal. These are integer, real, and string. We have already introduced the types used to represent numbers: integer and real.

- An integer can be represented in pure binary form. For example, the integer twenty five is represented as

$$1\ 1\ 0\ 0\ 1$$

- This kind of representation is called **radix** (or **positional**) **notation** In the decimal system the number

$$1\ 8\ 9$$

means

$$1 \times 10^2 + 8 \times 10^1 + 9 \times 10^0$$

Since 10^0 is 1 we speak of the hundreds position, the tens position, and the units position.

- In binary then the number 11001 is

$$1 \times 2^4 + 1 \times 2^3 + 0 \times 2^2 + 0 \times 2^1 + 1 \times 2^0$$

Since 2^4 is sixteen, and 2^3 is eight, and 2^0 is one, the number represented is twenty five as we said. It took five binary digits (bits) to represent the two-digit decimal number 25.

- In most computers a certain number of bits is reserved in the memory to store an integer. A common number is 32 bits.

- Bits are often grouped and the group is called a **byte**. In microcomputers there are 8 bits in a byte. It then takes 4 bytes to represent an integer of 32 bits. The more bytes used, the larger the integer that can be represented.

- Other computers may use a different number of bits in a byte.

• For real numbers you must store both the significant digits and also the position of the binary point. The binary point corresponds to the decimal point. This requires the storing of two integers. The integer representing the position of the binary point does not need as many bits as the integer representing the significant digits. A common number of bytes for a real number is a total of 8 bytes.

• Numbers can be positive or negative and the sign of a number can be represented by one bit, since it can only have one of two values: plus or minus.

• Another basic type of data that we will meet later is the **boolean** type. This type has only two values called **true** and **false**. A boolean variable could be represented by one bit. Boolean data cannot be input or output. If boolean variables are used, they must have their values given by an assignment statement.

Strings of Characters

In addition to the two kinds of numbers, integer and real, we can also store strings of **characters** in the computer's memory. These characters may be letters or digits, or special characters like asterisks and plus signs. A blank is also a character. To reserve memory space for holding a string of characters in a variable called *name*, we use this variable declaration

var name: string

The keyword **string** will cause enough space to be set aside for up to 256 characters of a string. The actual value stored is left-justified in this space. This means it is stored in the left-hand side of the 256 spaces available, with its first character in the first space on the left.

If we wanted to use a smaller amount of the memory, as we might later on when we store masses of data, we could use this type of declaration

var name: string (30)

which would reserve only space for 30 characters. When space in the memory is no problem, we just go ahead and use **string** without a space size in parentheses.

Here is a program to read in a person's name, both first and last, and output them with the last name first:

```
% The "lastfirst" program
% Reads first and last names and reverses them
var firstName, lastName: string
put "Enter your first name "..
get firstName
put "Enter your last name "..
get lastName
put "Name in reverse is ", lastName, ", ", firstName
```

Here is a sample execution window:

```
Enter your first name Alan
Enter your last name Turing
Name in reverse is Turing, Alan
```

The input prompt

```
put "Enter your first name" ..
```

has two dots after the output item. This means that the cursor is to stay in position right after the item is output and not go to the beginning of the next line. Notice also that when you enter a string for input, you do not need to put quotation marks around it as we did for string constants that we output.

The **put** statement that produces the last line of output could be replaced by these three statements:

```
put "Name in reverse is " ..
put lastName ..
put ", " ..
put firstName
```

Each of the first three have dots. The last one finishes the output line.

Token-oriented Input

Turing reads input strings as long as they are separated from each other by at least one blank or a return. A string of characters surrounded by what is called **white space** (blanks or return) is called a **token**. We say we have **token-oriented input** of strings.

The one character that must not be in the token is a blank. If an input string containing a blank is to be read as a token, it must be surrounded by quotation marks. Here is an example:

```
% The "name" program
% Reads a name and greets person
var name: string
put "Enter your full name in quotation marks"
get name
put "Hello ", name
```

Here is a sample execution window:

```
Enter your full name in quotation marks
"Albert Einstein"
Hello Albert Einstein
```

When an input token is surrounded by quotation marks the quotation marks are not stored in the memory. If you want to include a quotation mark in a string you must precede it with a **backslash**, namely \ . For example, the simple program

```
put "Say \"ah\""
```

will produce the output

```
Say "ah"
```

Strings Can Be Joined

In the *lastfirst* program we joined strings together in the output. We output the last name, a comma, then the first name. This can be carried out in the memory of the computer in this way:

```
var fullName: string
fullName := lastName + ", " + firstName
put fullName
```

In a sense the string for the first name has a comma added to it and then the last name is added. We use the operator + just as we did for adding numbers, but the meaning of adding strings is quite different from adding numbers. We are just joining strings together, end-to-end. Notice that the string constant in the joining operation has a comma followed by a blank.

Sometimes the joining can be done in the output and sometimes we use the join operator +. One reason for joining in the memory is to be able to see how long a string is produced. The function **length** can be used to determine how long a string actually is. For example,

```
% The "size" program
% Reads in a string and outputs its length
put "Enter a string"
var word : string
get word
put  "The word ", word, " has ", length (word), " letters"
```

Here is a sample execution window:

```
Enter a string
giraffe
The word giraffe has 7 letters
```

Selecting Part of a String

Just as strings can be joined together you can also select a part of a string. This part is called a **substring**. The positions of the characters in a string are numbered from the left. The numbers go from 1 to the length of the string. To select any one character of the string stored in a variable, you put its position number in parentheses after the string variable's name. For example, this program

var word: **string** := "splash"
put word (2)

would output the letter *p* which is the second letter of the string stored in the variable *word*.

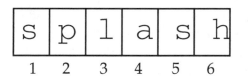

Notice that the variable *word* is given a value in the declaration. When this is done the data type could be omitted and we could have written the declaration this way:

var word := "splash"

If you want several successive characters from the string you would write

put word (2 .. 4)

In our example this would output *pla*, the second to the fourth character inclusive.

A special symbol * stands for the last character in the string. For this example

put word (*)

would output *h*, the last character of *splash*. The second last can be found in this way

put word (* − 1)

which would produce *s*.

You must be careful never to ask for a character position off either end of string. If you do, an error message will appear. For our example, either **put** *word (7)* or **put** *word (* − 7)* would produce error messages.

Codes for Characters

When strings of characters are stored in the computer, each character is stored in a coded form, often the **ASCII code**. The set of ASCII characters used by microcomputers is given in **Appendix 6**. Each character has a numerical value, for example, the character "A" is 65, "B" is 66, "C" is 67, and so on. Lower case letters have different values "a" is 97, "b" is 98, and so on. Here is a program that tells you what the numerical value of any character is:

```
% The "charval" program
% Gives numerical value of ASCII characters
var character: string (1)
put "Enter a single character "..
get character
put "ASCII value of ", character, " is ", ord (character)
```

The predefined function *ord* gives the order that the character you typed has in the ASCII sequence, that is its ASCII equivalent. Here is a sample execution window:

```
Enter a single character *
ASCII value of * is 42
```

There are 256 different ASCII characters whose values go from 0 to 255 inclusive. Here is a program to show you the character that corresponds to any one of these values:

```
% The "valchar" program
% Gives the ASCII character corresponding to its value
var value: int
put "Enter an integer between 0 and 255 "
get value
put "The character whose value is ", value, " is ",
     chr (value)
```

Here is a sample execution window:

```
Enter an integer between 0 and 255
64
The character whose value is 64 is @
```

Errors that you might make

- Forgetting the second quotation mark after a string constant: writing **put** "invoice.

- Trying to read a string containing a blank as a single token.

- Trying to use a quoted string containing a quotation mark: writing **put** "say "hello"".

- Trying to use a backslash as an ordinary character in a string. To output a single backslash you would write **put** "\\".

- Asking for a substring that contains a string position off the end of a string.

- Thinking the second last character of a string should be located by * – 2.

Problems

1.   Five words are to be input. The words are all to be entered on a single line with a variable number of spaces between them. You are to output them all on one line but with a single space between the words and then output the length of the line (including the spaces). Do this two different ways.

2.   Input a word and output its middle letter. If the word has an even number of characters, use the last character of the first half as the middle point.

3.   Input a word and output the last three characters. What happens if the word you input has only 2 characters?

4.   Write a program that asks you to enter a Capital letter and then outputs the corresponding little letter. For example, if you input *A* the output would be *a*.

5.   Write a program that asks you to enter a word and outputs the first and last letters joined together. For example, if you enter *pig* it outputs *pg*. What happens if you enter a one-letter word?

Questions for Discussion

1.   Can you see that the computer can multiply two integers faster than it can multiply two real numbers? Is this why we do not use real numbers for all our numerical calculations?

2.   A character like a backlash (\) is sometimes called an escape character – it allows you to escape from the normal sequence of a string. How do you include the backlash itself in the string as an ordinary character?

3.   What might happen if Turing did not give you an error message and refuse to go on with program execution when you ask for a character beyond the length of a string?

4.   We say Turing is a case sensitive language – it distinguishes between upper and lower case letters. Other programming languages, such as Basic let you use capital letters or little letters interchangeably. Is this an important difference?

Technical Terms you should now know

binary form
decimal form
digital computer
bit
representation of numbers
radix notation
byte
boolean
character
special character
string

white space
token
token-oriented input
backslash
join operator +
substring
ASCII code
ASCII value
ord
chr

Chapter 6

THE ELEMENTS OF PROGRAMMING: REPETITION

Before we can examine
the solution of more complicated problems
we must add to our repertoire
of elementary program constructs.

All the programs that we have had so far involve variable and constant declarations followed by a sequence of instructions that will be executed one after the other.

In the computer, the sequence of execution is handled by a part called the **control**. We say that the **control structure** of the program so far is **linear**.

There are two other control structures that will make up all our programs. These are called **repetition** and **selection**.

Before we can examine the solution of more complicated problems we must add to our repertoire of elementary program constructs.

In this chapter we will begin to look at repetition.

Questions and Answers about Repetition

Q.   Why should programs include repetition constructs?

A.   So the instructions can be used over and over.

Q.   Would the instructions be doing exactly the same thing each time they are repeated?

A.   No, that would just be a waste of time.

Q.   What is different from one execution of a repetition construct to the next?

A.   The values of certain variables must be changing.

Q.   How can we control the number of times repetition is to occur?

A.   Maybe you just want it to go on forever.

Q.   We'd call that an endless repetition. We'd be in an endless loop. How could you stop it?

A.   By turning the computer off.

Q.   Not a bad guess. But most programs can be stopped by something you do on the keyboard (or with the mouse if you have one). What other kinds of endings might you have for repetition?

A.   Maybe you could repeat until something happened to the variables that are changing with each repetition.

Q.   That would be a conditional loop – a certain condition would have to be true before you stopped the repetition. What other kind of repetition could there be?

A.   Repetition for a certain number of times, like 10 times.

Q.   That would be a counted loop. We will examine that in the next chapter.

Looping

The power of computers cannot be appreciated until you learn how to use a sequence of instructions over and over. This repeated use is sometimes called a **loop** because when you finish the last of the sequence of instructions in the loop you start back at the beginning of the loop.

Suppose you wanted to compute the cost of a series of items which must have a 15% sales tax added to their ticketed price.

This is a problem where we must be clear about what the problem is. Do we want the total cost of a number of such items or the cost including tax, of each one by itself? We ask the person who posed the problem to make the **problem specification** clearer. Suppose that what is wanted is the cost plus tax for each item individually. Here is a program that will do this for an indefinite series of purchases:

```
% The "costplus" program
% Compute the total cost including 15 percent tax
var cost, tax, total: real
const taxRate := 15.
loop
    put "cost= "..
    get cost
    % Compute tax to nearest cent
    tax := round (taxRate * cost) / 100
    total := cost + tax
    put "total cost= ", total
end loop
```

First of all, notice how the repetition is achieved. We surrounded the instructions to be executed repeatedly, once for each item purchased, by the keywords **loop** and **end loop**. The instructions between the keywords will then be repeated indefinitely until the user stops the execution of the program from the keyboard. The instructions between the keywords are indented 3 spaces. These form the **body of the loop**.

The instructions in this program are executed in the order shown in this flowchart. This is an infinite loop, which will keep running until you stop it with a special keyboard sequence. On an IBM PC compatible, this stopping sequence consists of holding down the Control key and pressing the Break key. On the Macintosh, it consists of holding down the Apple (command) key and pressing a period.

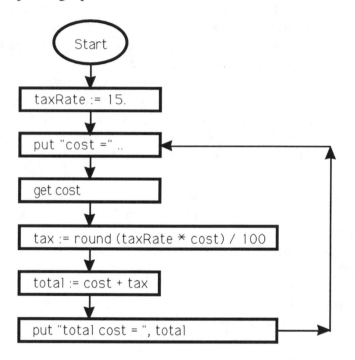

Several points should be noted:

- We started the program with two comments, the first giving the program a name, the second saying what the program does.

- The known quantity is *cost*, the unknowns *tax* and *total*. The *taxRate* is also known and is constant. When we use a variable name that is really two words, like taxRate, we often capitalize the first letter of the second word. Turing distinguishes between **upper** and **lower case** letters so we must be careful to be consistent and not try to refer to the constant as *taxrate*. Using *taxrate* would produce an error message indicating an undeclared variable. We say Turing is **case sensitive**.

- The input prompt was written with two dots after it. This causes the cursor to remain on the same line as the prompt so that the value for *cost* can be input there.

- Since we must compute the tax to the nearest cent with a rather complicated instruction, we precede it with a comment to say what is happening.

- The quantity *taxRate * cost* will produce a value in cents for the tax. This quantity has a real value and will, in general have a fractional part. We want to round off the tax to the nearest cent. Using *round (taxRate * cost)* does this. We then divide the number of cents by 100 to express it as dollars and cents.

- We could have written the program without introducing either of the variables *tax* and *total* by writing as the output instruction

    put "total cost= ", cost + round (taxRate * cost) / 100

    This program would not be as easy to understand. That is why we often introduce **intermediate variables**.

Here is a sample execution window

```
cost= 5.00
total cost= 5.75
cost= 11.25
total cost= 12.94
cost=
```

The execution has been interrupted after the third input prompt .

Testing Programs

To test whether the program is giving correct results, you should do these calculations on your hand calculator to check that they are the same. The result for a cost of 5.00 dollars is easy, since the tax is exactly 75 cents. For the second case, where the cost is 11.25 dollars, the tax will be 168.75 cents. This is rounded off to 169 cents or 1.69 dollars. The total cost will be 12.94 dollars which agrees with the computer's result.

All programs should be tested with a variety of different values of the input variables. We call these **test values** If you compare the computer's results with calculators to check that they agree you can be confident that, when you use the program to find values not check by hand, these too will be correct.

Testing programs uncovers errors but it can never prove that the program is **correct**, that is, will give correct results in all cases. Errors are called **bugs**. Looking for errors is called **debugging**.

Sometimes when you are developing a program you need to know what is happening between output instructions. You can investigate this by inserting additional output instructions into your program during testing. You can remove these added output instructions later when you are satisfied with the program. For example, in our program we could insert the instruction

```
put "tax=",  tax
```

right after the value is assigned to *tax*. This would let us see what is computed. It is a good idea to label what you are outputting so it is easy to understand.

Labelling of Tables

When we have single values the practice of prompting each input and labelling each output is a natural one. When there is repetition we often use the form of a **table** where the similar values are in columns and the columns have headings. For example, in the previous program we might have headings with columns of output

```
cost    total
5.00     5.75
11.25    12.94
```

To get this result we must know how to space the results in a line.

When we give a **put** instruction we can specify the size of a **field** (number of columns) that we want the output to occupy. This field size is given, after a colon, following the output item itself. When a number is output in a field it is placed at the right-hand side of the field. We say it is **right justified**.

When strings are output in a field they are **left justified**. For example, the output instruction

> **put** "2 + 2 is": 10, 2 + 2: 5, "cm.": 5

would produce this output (the spaces are shown as a ◇)

```
2◇+◇2◇is◇◇◇◇◇◇4cm.◇◇
```

Here we have drawn boxes around each output character, so it is easy to count the number of characters in each output field.

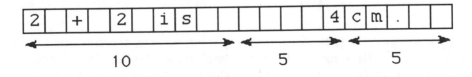

The first string is left justified in a field of size 10 which produces two blanks after the *is*. The number 4 is right justified in the field of size 5 which produces four more blanks before the 4. Since the second string is left justified, its field size is irrelevant. You must choose field sizes to produce a pleasing spacing. It is probably easier here not to use field sizes at all, but include any blanks we want in the strings themselves with this output instruction

put "2 + 2 is ", 2 + 2," cm."

Whenever you want results in a table you must **format** the output with field sizes. Here is the *costplus* program rewritten with the values given as a table:

```
% The "cost2" program
% Compute the total cost including 15 percent tax
var cost, tax, total: real
const taxRate := 15.
% Output heading to table
put "cost":10, "total"
loop
    get cost
    % Compute tax to nearest cent
    tax := round (taxRate * cost) / 100
    total := cost + tax
    put total: 15: 2
end loop
```

Here is a sample execution window:

```
cost        total
5.00
            5.75
11.25
            12.94
```

Because we must press the Return key after we enter the cost, the total cost cannot be on the same line but will appear on the next line. We specified the format for *total* as 15 spaces but then added a second colon, and a 2. This

2 controls the number of **decimal places** we want to be output. The value will thus be rounded off to the nearest cent on output. Still, we might have left the result for the tax unrounded. If you are keeping track of the total tax on all the items then you would have to keep the tax on each purchase rounded in the computer's memory.

The input values for *cost* are positioned in the table when the user enters the values are entered on the keyboard.

Stopping a Loop

We were able to terminate the execution of the *costplus* program from the keyboard. Sometimes we do this by entering a special item of input data, one that is not normal. For example, we could enter a negative value for the cost. If we insert an instruction in the *costplus* program just after the **get** *cost* instruction namely

exit when cost < 0

we will **exit**, or leave, the loop and go to the instruction following **end loop** when a negative value of cost is input (the < means is less than). Since there are no instructions after the **end loop**, the program will terminate. We could add this instruction after **end loop**

put "The End"

Here is the flow chart for our modified program.

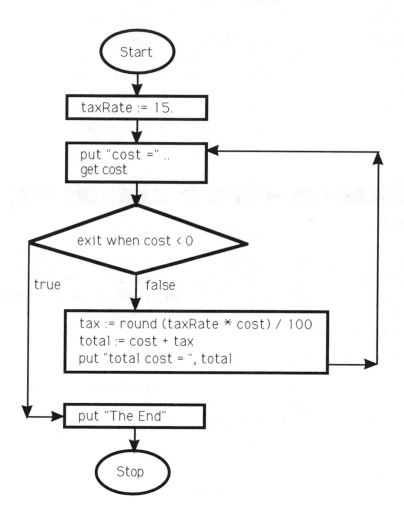

Now an execution window might be:

```
        cost= 1.00
        total cost= 1.15
        cost= 2.00
        total cost= 2.30
        cost= −1.00
        The End
```

Notice that you leave the loop just as soon as the negative cost is read. Such a value is referred to as a **sentinel** or **end-of-file** value.

A loop that has an **exit when** is a **conditional loop**. It ends when the **condition** is **true**.

Conditions

A simple condition expresses the relation between two quantities. The condition may be either true or false. The simple condition is in the form

expression comparison-operator expression

The set of **comparison operators** is:

=	equal to
<	less than
>	greater than
not=	not equal to
<=	less than or equal
>=	greater than or equal

- The expressions must be of the same kind of data type, that is, a number (**int** or **real**), or a **string**. If they are not of the same type, an error message will result. To be equal, two strings must be of the same length.

- **Compound conditions** can be created by combining simple conditions with **logical operators** in the form

  ### condition logical-operator condition

- With the logical operator **and** the compound condition is true only if both conditions are true. With the logical operator **or** the compound condition is true if either or both of the conditions are true.

- The logical operator **not** can be used in front of any condition to reverse its true and false value. For example,

  ### not 5 > 4

  has a value false since the condition 5 > 4 is true. This is somewhat confusing so we seldom use **not** except in **not=**.

Errors that you might make

- Not testing a program on a wide enough range of test values.

- Not lining up the headings of columns properly in an output table.

- Not rounding to the nearest cent in the computer memory when amounts are to be accumulated as they are with bank interest.

- Not remembering how to stop an endless loop.

- Forgetting the **end loop** statement.

- Trying to test two real numbers to see if they are equal. Real numbers often are close to equal but not exactly so.

- Trying to compare an integer with a string. For example, 25 < "26".

- Mixing up the < and > comparison operators.

- Using => instead of >=.

- Using =< instead of <=.

- Placing the **exit when** in the wrong place in a conditional loop.

- Not knowing where to insert extra output instructions in a program so as to follow the details of execution during the debugging phase.

- Forgetting to label the values that are output by additional output instructions.

Questions for Discussion

1.   Which of these simple conditions is true?

    a. 5 <= 6
    b. 7 not= 5
    c. "a" > "b"
    d. "a" > "A"
    e. "stop" = "stop"
    f. "Bill" = "BILL"
    g. "stop " = "stop"
    h. 8 **div** 2 = 4
    i. 8 / 2 <= 4
    j. 10 **mod** 3 = 1
    k. "Bill" > "bill"

2.   Which of these compound conditions is true?

    a. (5 > 6) **or** (7 > 6)
    b. (2 + 2 = 4) **and** (7 – 3 < 5)
    c. (2 + 3 **not**= 5) **or** (3 + 1 < 6)
    d. (6 < 7) **or** (5 > 2)
    e. (6 < 7) **and** (5 > 2)

3.   Why is it important to round values stored in the computer to the nearest cent in a banking application?

4.   If you have a daily interest account in a bank, how often must the interest be calculated? What about weekends?

5.   Should it matter very much whether the sales tax is computed on each individual item and then added up or on the total cost in one calculation?

6.   Why is the way the results of a computer program are to be displayed often not a part of the problem specification?

7.   Why must we use output formatting with field sizes when results are to be in a table?

Problems

Write programs that meet the specifications of the problem in each of these.

1.   Find the average mark in an examination for a number students whose exam marks are entered on the keyboard one after the other. Use an end-of-file sentinel.

2.   Find the total cost of a series of items and compute the tax on these to the nearest cent if the tax rate is 7%. Do not compute the tax on each item just on the total.

3.   Write a program to output the square of integers starting at 5 and going up by 5s. Stop when the square becomes larger than 5000. Tabulate the results with proper headings.

4.   Write a program for a bank savings account. The bank pays 6% interest annually and you deposit $1000 at the beginning of each year. How many years must you do this before your bank balance is larger than $10,000.00? Be sure to round the interest to the nearest cent.

5.   A homeowner takes out a mortgage for $120,000 at 9.5% per year. At the end of each year an amount of $24,000 is paid. Write a program to show how the mortgage is paid off, year by year, until nothing is owing.

Technical Terms you should now know

control structure
linear sequence
repetition
selection
loop
problem specification
loop
end loop
body of loop
lower case
upper case
case sensitive
round off
round
testing of program
test values
correctness of program
program bug

debugging
formatting of output
field size
right justified
left justified
table of results
decimal place
exit when
sentinel
end-of-file value
conditional loop
simple condition
comparison operator
compound condition
logical operator
and
or
not

Chapter 7

THE ELEMENTS OF PROGRAMMING: COUNTED REPETITION

*Counted repetition is an extremely
useful construct although, in fact,
we could get along without it.*

In the last chapter we introduced the repetition construct.

The part of a program that you want to execute repeatedly is enclosed by the keywords **loop** and **end loop**.

If the loop is not to be executed endlessly, there must be an instruction inside the loop body that causes control to exit from the loop. This exit instruction contains a condition so the loop is called a conditional loop. We exit when a certain condition is true.

There is a second kind of repetition construct that arranges for the loop to be repeated a fixed number of times; the repetitions are counted.

Counted repetition is an extremely useful construct although, in fact, we could get along without it.

Questions and Answers about Counted Repetition

Q.   How is a counted loop to be controlled?

A.   By having a counter.

Q.   The counter is called the **index** of the loop. Where will the value of the index at any time be stored?

A.   In the memory of the computer.

Q.   How do we reserve memory space for the index?

A.   By declaring its name as a variable in the program in a declaration.

Q.   That is not quite the way we do it. You will see. We will declare it by simply mentioning its name in the key line that starts the loop. What other information would you expect in the key line?

A.   The number of times the loop is to be repeated. You would count them.

Q.   How would you count 10 repetitions?

A.   Well 1, 2, 3, 4, 5, 6, 7, 8, 9, 10.

Q.   How about 100?

A.   I'd count 1, 2, and so on up to 100.

Q.   We write that as 1 .. 100. Do you always count up by ones starting at 1?

A.   When I count seconds I count 1001, 1002, and so on. You count rockets backwards 10, 9, 8, ... and so on. I counted by 5's for hide and seek as a kid: 5, 10, 15, 20, and so on.

Q.   We can use all these ways in counted repetition.

Counted Repetition

Frequently we want to repeat a process a fixed number of times rather than until some condition is true. For these we use a repetition construct called a **counted loop**. Here is a flow chart for a program which contains a counted loop.

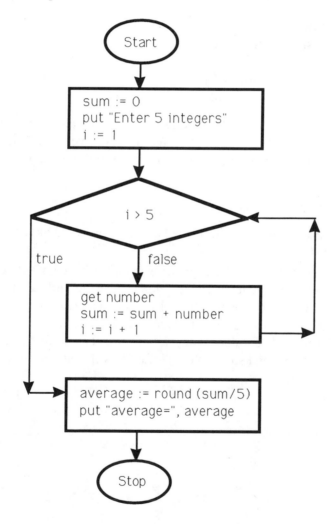

Here is the program that will read 5 integers and output their average to the nearest integer.

```
% The "avgfive" program
% Compute the average of 5 integers
var number, average: int
var sum : int := 0
put "Enter 5 integers"
for count: 1 .. 5
    get number
    sum := sum + number
end for
average := round (sum / 5)
put "average = ", average
```

In this example the variable *sum* is declared as an integer variable and in the declaration it is given an integer value of 0. We do not have to include the data type in the declaration when a variable is **initialized** in the declaration. We could have written

```
var sum := 0
```

If *sum* were to be a **real** variable and initialized to zero, we would have to put a decimal point after the zero.

The counted loop starts with the keyword **for** and ends with **end for**. After the **for** we name an integer variable *count* to be the **index** of the counted loop. The **range** of the count is from 1 to 5 in that sequence. So the **body of the loop**, the set of instructions between the keywords **for** and **end for**, is executed 5 times. The value of the index *count* is 1 on the first execution, 2 on the second, and so on. You can see this if you output *count* by including the instruction

```
put count
```

just after the **get** instruction.

Here is a sample execution window.

```
    Enter 5 integers
6
1
3
2
7
3
5
4
1
5
    average = 4
```

If you enter all the numbers on one line before the return, this is what the execution window would look like.

```
    6 3 7 5 1
1
2
3
4
5
    average = 4
```

The value of *count* is not available outside the loop body, so if you ask for its value after the loop is finished, you will get an error message saying that it is an undeclared variable. We say that *count* is **local** to the loop. Note that *count* is, in fact, not declared in a **var** declaration. Its appearance after the keyword **for** automatically declares it as an integer variable.

Doing Without the Counted Loop

We said that although the counted loop is useful we could, in fact, get along without it. Here is a program that does exactly what the *avgfive* program does, but uses a conditional loop instead :

```
% The "avg5" program
% Compute the average of 5 integers
% Using a conditional loop construct
var number, average: int
var count, sum: int := 0
put "Enter 5 integers"
loop
    count := count + 1
    exit when count > 5
    get number
    sum := sum + number
end loop
average := round (sum / 5)
put "average = ", average
```

Here the integer counter *count* must be declared and initialized outside the loop. In the loop, *count* is increased by 1 each time around. The **exit when** stops the repetition when *count* becomes 6.

The counted loop handles the incrementing of the index automatically and is easier to understand. That is why it is convenient, but not essential, to have counted repetitions as a construct in a programming language.

Counting Backwards and by Steps

Counted loops usually go up by ones or down by ones. If you want a loop to count down by ones you use this form

for decreasing count: 5 .. 1

In this case the values of *count* are 5, 4, 3, 2, 1, in turn.

You can also go up or down by steps other than ones . To do this, you give the range of the number, then the keyword **by**, and then the step size. All of this happens within the **for** instruction. The **for** instruction

for count 1 .. 7 **by** 2

will cause the values of *count* to be 1, 3, 5, 7.

1. A mortgage of $100,000 being held at an annual rate of 11.5% is paid off by annual installments of $15,000. Produce a table of results showing the balance owing at the beginning of the year, the interest due at the end, and the new balance after the payment is received for the first 20 years. Was the mortgage paid off?

2. A person deposits $1,000 at the beginning of every year in a savings account that has 7% annual interest. Output a table showing the balance in the account at the end of each year for 10 years.

3. A bank offers a daily interest account with a rate of 5 / 365 percent each day, compounded daily. What annual rate is this equivalent to?

4. What amount of money must you deposit in the bank at the beginning of a year so that you will have $1000.00 at the end, if the annual interest is 6 percent.

5.   Input a series of words ending with 'stop' and output each of them in turn with their letters in reverse order.

Graphical Examples of Counted Loops

We can output a character at any point in the execution window by using the instruction

locate (row, column)

before we give the output instruction. For the PC, in the execution window there are 25 rows each containing 80 columns. You can output a maximum of 80 characters on a line and a maximum of 25 lines. Here is a program that places a vertical line of asterisks in column 10, going from row 5 to row 10 inclusive:

```
% The "vertical" program
% Draw a vertical line of asterisks
const column := 10
for row: 5 .. 10
    locate (row, column)
    put "*" ..
end for
```

When we want to output characters in a graphical form we always use two dots after the output instruction. If we do not do this the **put** instruction will fill out the line with blanks. This might erase something we have already output.

Here is a diagram of the program's output.

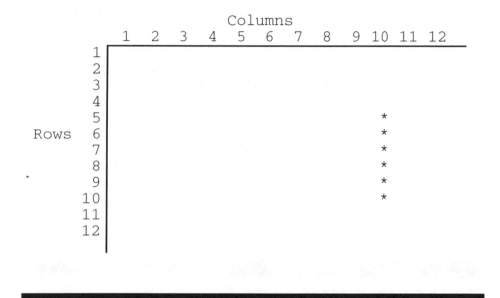

![Black bar]

Loops Nested inside Loops

Here is a program that draws a rectangle, completely filled with asterisks by drawing a series of vertical lines as before, starting in column 10 and going to column 40:

```
% The "block" program
% Draw a block of asterisks bounded
% by columns 10 and 40 and rows 5 and 20
for column: 10 .. 40
    for row: 5 .. 20
        locate (row, column)
        put "*" ..
    end for
end for
```

In the **put** instruction, we again use two dots after the asterisk so that the line is not wiped out. When counted loops are nested, we indent the body of the second loop another three spaces beyond the body of the first. This is called **paragraphing** the program, and can be done automatically in the Turing Editor.

Nested loops must not have the same index variable. For example, this program has a syntax error because each of the nested loops is trying to use the same index *i*.

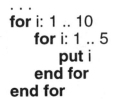

```
. . .
for i: 1 .. 10
   for i: 1 .. 5
      put i
   end for
end for
```

Changing the Colors on the Screen

If you have a color screen on your computer you can display characters in color by giving the instruction

```
color (colorNumber)
```

where for the PC the *colorNumber* can range from 0 to 15. All characters displayed will have this color until a different color instruction is given. In Turing *color* can also be spelled as *colour*. The exact colors are given in the appendix for your computer. For the PC, if 16 is added to the color number the color will blink. Here are three colors to use: blue has color number 1, red has 4, white has 7, and black 0.

The background can also be colored by using

```
colorback (colorNumber)
```

Background colors for the PC have numbers from 0 to 7.

How to Repeat a String

In Turing the predefined function

repeat (pattern, howMany)

produces as a value a string of characters in which the *pattern* is repeated *howMany* times in the line. For example, to produce a row of 80 asterisks right across the screen in row 5 use these instructions:

```
locate (5, 1)
put repeat ("*", 80)
```

Here is a program that fills the whole screen with diagonal lines of red slashes on a blue background:

```
% The "twill" program
% Fill screen with diagonal lines
% of red asterisks on a blue background
const red := 4
const blue := 1
colorback (blue)
color (red)
for count: 1 .. 12
    locate (2 * count – 1, 1)
    put repeat ("/ ", 40)
end for
for count: 1 .. 12
    locate (2 * count, 1)
    put repeat (" /", 40)
end for
```

Here is the pattern produced by the program.

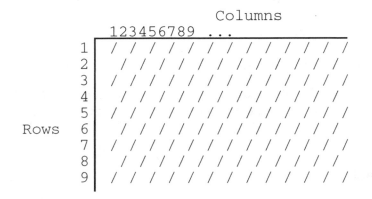

In the pattern every other row is the same. The first pattern is 40 repetitions of a slash followed by a blank. The second pattern is 40 repetitions of a blank followed by a slash. There are 13 rows of the first pattern and 12 of the second. The index *count* is used for each of the **for** loops which is alright here since one is not nested inside the other.

In this program the index variable *count*, which is counting the number of similar lines, is used to compute the row number for the output. For the first **for** loop the row number is given as

2 * count − 1

When *count* = 1, this has a value 1, that is row 1. When *count* = 2 the row number is 3. The odd-numbered rows are all the same. When *count* is 13 the row number is 25. You should always check the end values of any loop to see that they produce the values you expect. The row numbers for the other pattern will be 2, 4, ..., 24, even-numbered rows ending with 24.

Problems

Use color in these graphical problems if you have a color screen.

1.   Write a program that will draw a diagonal line of asterisks from the first row, first column to the 25th row, 25th column. (Use a counted loop.)

2.   Write a program that draws a diagonal line of asterisks from the 25th row, first column to the first row, 25th column. (Again use a counted loop.)

3.   Write a program that draws a diagonal line of asterisks from row 1, column 1 to row 25, column 25. (Use a conditional loop)

4.   Write a program to draw an outlined rectangle of asterisks whose upper-left and lower-right corners are to be given by the user.

5.   Write a program to draw a rectangle filled with asterisks whose upper-left and lower-right corners are to be given by the user.

6.   See if you can write a program that does any one of the things in the previous problems but uses the **loop** ... **end loop** repetition construct rather than a counted loop.

An Exit in a Counted Loop

You can combine the properties of a counted loop with a conditional loop by using an **exit when** in the body of the counted loop.

Here is the program that reads words and repeats them (**echoes** them) until it has read 10 words or until it reads the word "stop". It outputs the number of words before "stop".

```
% The "tenwords" program
% Reads a maximum of 10 words
% unless it reads the word "stop"
var word: string
put "Enter words one to a line"
var count: int := 0
for howMany: 1 .. 10
    get word
    exit when word = "stop"
    put word
    count := howMany
end for
put "You read ", count, " words before 'stop'"
```

Here is a sample execution window:

```
Enter words one to a line
ball
ball
top
top
stop
You read 2 words before 'stop'
```

Notice that "stop" is not echoed or counted since the exit occurs right after it has been read. The maximum number it would read would be 10. In the loop we stored the value of the index *howMany* in a variable named *count.* Outside the loop, after the exit, *count* will record the last value of *howMany* before the "stop" is read. Remember we cannot output the value of *howMany* itself once we leave the loop. Why is the value of *count* initialized to zero in its declaration?

In this example we are reading a series of strings. Remember that strings read as tokens need not be put in quotation marks, but must be surrounded by white space (returns or blanks).

Errors that you might make

- Not putting a colon before the range in a counted loop: writing

  for count 1 .. 10

- Declaring the index of a counted loop.

- Trying to output the value of the index of a loop after the loop has finished executing.

- Forgetting to include the **end for** of a counted loop.

- Confusing the value 0 and 0. when initializing a variable in a declaration when the data type is omitted.

- Trying to change the value of the index of a counted loop by an assignment statement.

- Counting one too many or one too few in a counted loop.

- Forgetting to show the range in a **for decreasing** loop with the lower value first. For example,

  for decreasing count: 1 .. 5

- Reversing the order of the two parameters when using the predefined function *repeat*: using **put** repeat (5, "*").

- Using the same name for the index in two nested loops.

Problems

The problems marked with an asterisk are more mathematial.

1.   Write a program that counts backwards by 5s. Start counting at 100. Before you start counting ask for a number to be input. When the count would be less than the input number, stop counting.

2.   Write a program that asks the user to enter a row and column and then draws a line of asterisks from that location diagonally downward to the right until it hits the edge of the window at the bottom or at the side.

*3.   Write a program that computes the value of the series

$$1 + x + x^2 + x^3 + x^4 \ldots$$

for any value of x that is less than one. Stop adding terms in the series when the contribution of the term to be added next is less then .0001.

*4.   Write a program to calculate the value of *factorialn* for values of n going from 1 to 50. Remember:

> *Factorial* 3 is $3 \times 2 \times 1$
> *Factorial* 8 is $8 \times 7 \times 6 \times 5 \times 4 \times 3 \times 2 \times 1$

What is the expression for *factorial n*? Is your calculation as efficient as it can be?

Hint: you should use real numbers in the calculation and compute each successive factorial from the previous one. What is the relationship between *factorial (n)* and *factorial (n–1)*? Tabulate the results.

Questions for Discussion

1.   How does paragraphing programs help to make them more understandable?

2.   Could the "twill" program of this chapter be done using counted loops with steps of 2?

3.   Some programming languages do not allow a conditional exit from a counted loop. What would you have to do to get this result in such languages?

4.   Why does Turing have the restriction (which is not in other languages) that you may not alter the index of a counted loop by a statement in the loop?

5.   Why is the value of the index of a counted loop not available outside the loop body?

Technical Terms you should now know

counted loop	color in graphics
initialization in declaration	color monitor
index of counted loop	*colorNumber*
decreasing	*colorback*
step size	background color
by	function
character graphics	*repeat*
locate	echo input
nested loop	string input
paragraphing program	token

Chapter 8

A SYSTEMATIC METHOD FOR PROBLEM SOLVING

. . . there is no such thing as
a set of all purpose rules
for problem solving.

This is a book on problem solving.

We have looked at problems that are not problems because we remember the answers.

We also saw how we could solve a more general problem by first solving particular instances of the problem.

In the last two chapters we added to our computer knowledge by seeing how programs could handle repetition.

We return now to the problem of "how to solve problems". The most important point to realize is that there is no such thing as a set of all purpose rules for problem solving.

In this chapter we will look at one systematic method for solving problems. This method is useful for many different types of problems that can be addressed by computer programs.

A Systematic Method

- *Understand what the problem is.*
  Decide what information you are being given, in the problem specification or to be supplied by the user – the **knowns**. Also decide what information you are to compute and produce as output – the **unknowns**.

- *Give names to the knowns and the unknowns.*
  Decide what data type each of them is to be, so that later you can produce the program declarations.

- *Determine the relationships between the unknowns and knowns.*
  Express these relationships in a mathematical form for precision. This is known as developing an **algorithm** for computing.

- *Decide whether any intermediate values must be computed.*

- *Decide whether there are any constants to be used in the calculations.*

- *Decide how the results are to be displayed.*

- *Devise the program.*
  Create the data declarations for variables and constants and express the algorithm as a series of instructional steps. For complicated algorithms the algorithm might have to be developed step-by-step rather than simply as a series of Turing instructions. The intermediate steps would involve a gradual transition from the expression of what is to be done in English, to a mixture of English and Turing, then finally to the Turing program.

- *Run the program on test data and compare the results with hand calculations.*

- *Assess whether there are more efficient algorithms for producing the same result.*
  This step is unnecessary in many cases.

- *Determine whether the program is correct.*
  Have all the problem specifications been satisfied?

- *Decide whether the program could be made more general.*
  This is a question we might ask if we think we have created a generally useful solution.

Example Problem to be Solved

- *Problem specification:*
  Prepare a multiplication table showing the products of all integers from 1 to 10 inclusive. There are 100 values to be calculated and displayed.

- *Understand the problem*
  You must produce a "times" table which will be a 10 by 10 table in which the 10 column headings are integers from 1 to 10 inclusive and whose rows are labelled with the same set of integers. The table entries are the products of the column headings and the row headings. The headings are the knowns, the products are the unknowns.

- *Name the knowns and unknowns*
  We will call the column headings the *multiplier* and the row headings the *multiplicand*. These will be knowns. We will call the unknowns *product*.

- *Data types of knowns and unknowns*
  They will all be of the data type integer.

- *Relationships between knowns and unknowns*
  The relationship is

$$\text{product} = \text{multiplier} \times \text{multiplicand}$$

- *Intermediate values*
  There are none.

- *Constants*
  There are none.

- *Display of results*

  There will be headings on each of the 10 columns showing the values of the multiplier and opposite each of the 10 rows showing the values of the multiplicand. The products will be displayed in fields of size 5 spaces. This will require a total of 50 spaces plus 5 for the row heading. Here is what the table looks like:

```
            1     2     3     4     5     6     7     8     9    10
      1     1     2     3     4     5     6     7     8     9    10
      2     2     4     6     8    10    12    14    16    18    20
      3     3     6     9    12    15    18    21    24    27    30
      4     4     8    12    16    20    24    28    32    36    40
      5     5    10    15    20    25    30    35    40    45    50
      6     6    12    18    24    30    36    42    48    54    60
      7     7    14    21    28    35    42    49    56    63    70
      8     8    16    24    32    40    48    56    64    72    80
      9     9    18    27    36    45    54    63    72    81    90
     10    10    20    30    40    50    60    70    80    90   100
```

- *Devise the program*

  We will first describe the program in English mixed with some Turing, then refine the program into Turing alone. We will use nested counted loops whose indexes give the values of the *multiplier* and *multiplicand*. Since the products must be output by rows, the index of the outer loop will be the row number, the *multiplicand*, and the index of the inner loop the column number, the *multiplier*. We will need to put column headings across the top and row headings down the side. Here is the program:

```
% The "times" program
% Produces a 10 by 10 multiplication table
var product: int
% Output headings of columns
put "": 5 ..
for multiplier: 1 .. 10
    put multiplier: 5 ..
end for
put ""
for multiplicand: 1 .. 10
    % Output row heading
```

```
        put multiplicand: 5 ..
        % Output products in row
        for multiplier: 1 .. 10
                product := multiplier * multiplicand
                put product: 5 ..
        end for
        put ""
    end for
```

Notice that the rows, both the heading row and the rows of the table, are finished by the instruction **put** "" which will cause a new line to be started.

- *Run the program on test data and check with hand calculator*
  Here there are no input values so we simply run the program and check a few of the results by inspection. (In this case, we assume that you know your times tables and know the answers already.)

- *Assess whether there is a more efficient algorithm*
  We could have used a method of addition rather than multiplication to produce the product values. Since on some computers addition takes less time than multiplication, using addition take less computer time and therefore would be more efficient. The inner loop of the program would be this:

```
    product := multiplicand
    for multiplier: 1 .. 10
    put product: 5 ..
            product := product + multiplicand
    end for
```

We will look later at a method for experimentally comparing the efficiency of the two algorithms by timing the calculations. It is only when we are repeating the same type of calculations many times that we care about making the calculations efficient. That is why we said that this step is unncessary in many cases.

- *Have the problem specifications been satisfied?*
  We have a labelled 10 by 10 table of products which is what we were asked to produce.

- *Could the program be made more general?*
  We could read in the ranges of values for the multiplier and multiplicand and produce a different multiplication table. We would have to be careful if a larger than 10 by 10 table was to be produced. With 80 columns available and 5 spaces for each product we could accommodate a table that is up to 15 by 10 with headings, but no larger. If the products become larger than 5 digits there would be trouble too. If a field size is specified that is too small the computer will just use a larger one as needed.

Tracing the Execution of a Program

In this example we have omitted the step about deciding whether or not the program is correct. It is true that we compared the results with hand calculations and, since we knew what they should be, we could check every result.

In most programs we can not check every result. In fact, there is no point to using the computer when we know every result before we start as we do here. The multiplication table has just been an example to illustrate the formal method of problem solving for computers. In most problems we can check only a small sample of test values and from there on, hope the other values are correct.

The ideal is to be able to prove mathematically that a program will give the right result for all cases. This is a complicated procedure and involves some very sophisticated mathematical reasoning and will not be discussed in this book.

We have a second-best method of trying to see if a program is correct and that is by tracing its execution by hand. In this method we pretend we are the computer and execute the instructions one-by-one. As each instruction is executed we write down what values are stored in each variable including the indexes of any loops.

We will now trace the execution of the supposedly more efficient algorithm for the multiplication table. Here the trace is useful because it is not obvious that the program will produce correct results. Tracing is usually done before you run the program on the computer and is a good way to get rid of many errors right away.

Here is the program we will trace:

```
% The "newtimes" program
% Produces a 10 by 10 multiplication table
% without using any computer multiplication
% Output headings of columns
put "": 5 ..
for multiplier: 1 .. 10
    put multiplier: 5 ..
end for
put ""
for multiplicand: 1 .. 10
    % Output row heading
    put multiplicand: 5 ..
    % Output products in row
    var product := multiplicand
    for multiplier: 1 .. 10
        put product: 5 ..
        product := product + multiplicand
    end for
    put ""
end for
```

It is easy enough to see by inspection without formal tracing that the first part of the program, which produces the column headings is correct. We will concentrate on the remainder of the program and show the values of the variable *product* and index variables *multiplicand* and *multiplier* just at the stage where the instruction

put product: 5 ..

is to be executed each time.

multiplicand	multiplier	product
1	1	1
1	2	2
1	3	3
1	4	4
1	...	...
1	10	10
2	1	2
2	2	4
2	3	6
2	...	...
2	10	20
	...	...

You should trace execution long enough so that you are confident that the results are correct. When loops are present, you should check the first and last execution of the body of the loop to see that they produce correct results. In this case the last execution of the outer loop is:

multiplicand	multiplier	product
10	1	10
10	2	20
10	3	30
...	...	...
10	10	100

which is the correct result.

Satisfying the Problem Specification

We have not looked directly at the results to see that all problem specifications have been satisfied.

Here are the specifications again:

Prepare a multiplication table showing the products of all integers from 1 to 10 inclusive. There are 100 values to be calculated and displayed.

On reviewing the specifications we see that they have been satisfied and that the results are "correct" as far as we can tell. The display of results as far as field sizes and spacing was not described in detail and we added that part of the specification ourselves. Usually you would check with the person proposing the problem to see if the form you propose will be suitable to them. Often they have not thought this part out and a certain amount of consultation is required to fill in the details.

Another Example of the Systematic Method

Here is the *problem specification:*

Output a calender for any month where you are given the name of the month, the number of days in the month, and the number of the day of the week when the first of the month occurs. The first day of the week is taken as Sunday.

- *Understand the problem*
  The knowns are the name of the month, the starting day of week, and the length of the month. We must produce a labelled table of dates with 7 columns and a number of rows which may be spread over as little as 4 or as many as 6 weeks.

- *Name the unknowns and the knowns*
  We will call the knowns *month, monthLength,* and *startDay.* The unknown is the *dateNumber.*

- *Data type of knowns and unknowns*
  They will all be of the data type integer except for *month* which will be of type string.

- *Relationship between the knowns and the unknowns*
  In the first week *startDay* is the day of *dateNumber* = 1. The other dates follow sequentially with day 1 following each day 7.

- *Intermediate values*
  None.

- *Constants*
  Days in week, names of days in week.

- *Display of results*
  There will be headings giving: the name of the month centered, then on the next line the day of the week. We will allow 8 spaces for each day using 3 letter abbreviations for the day names. The dates should line up under the day names.

  Here is an example calendar for January. In this case the first day of the month falls on a Tuesday.

```
                     January
     Sun      Mon      Tue      Wed      Thu      Fri      Sat
                        1        2        3        4        5
      6        7        8        9       10       11       12
     13       14       15       16       17       18       19
     20       21       22       23       24       25       26
     27       28       29       30       31
```

- *Devise the program*
  We will break the problem up into 4 parts.

  Input the month name, month length, and start day
  Output the calendar heading
  Output the dates in the first week
  Output the dates in the remaining weeks

We can now refine this into a Turing program. We will keep this first sketch as comments in the final program. Here is the program:

```
% The "calendar" program
% Input month name, month length and start day
% and produce a calendar for the month
var monthName: string
var startDay, monthLength: int
const day1 := "Sun"
const day2 := "Mon"
const day3 := "Tue"
const day4 := "Wed"
```

```
const day5 := "Thu"
const day6 := "Fri"
const day7 := "Sat"
% Input month, length, and start day
put "Enter name of month "..
get monthName
put "Enter month length " ..
get monthLength
put "Enter starting day number, Sun is 1 " ..
get startDay
% Output the calendar heading
put "": 20, monthName
put "": 5, day1: 8, day2: 8, day3: 8, day4: 8,
        day5: 8, day6: 8, day7: 8
% Output the dates in the first week
for day: 1 .. startDay −1
    put "": 8 ..
end for
var dateNumber := 1
for day: startDay .. 7
    put dateNumber: 8 ..
    dateNumber := dateNumber + 1
end for
put ""
% Output dates in remaining weeks
loop
    for day: 1 .. 7
        put dateNumber: 8 ..
        dateNumber := dateNumber + 1
        exit when dateNumber > monthLength
    end for
    put ""
    exit when dateNumber > monthLength
end loop
```

In the last section of the program for outputting the dates in remaining weeks both the inner and outer loops have conditional exits when the *dateNumber* becomes greater than the month length.

- *Correctness of the program.*

  We should perhaps trace the execution of the program for several extreme cases where the start day is mid-week, where it is on Sunday, and where the end day is Saturday. We can check the first and last case together if we take the month of October which starts on Thursday (day 5) and has 31 days.

  We will trace the first part of the program. The first **for** loop outputs a blank of width eight spaces from days 1 to 4. The next **for** loop outputs the dates 1, 2, 3, for *day* going from 5 to 7 and leaves *dateNumber* with the value 4 as it enters the last part of the program with the nested loops. The first execution of the outer loop will result in dates 4, 5, 6, 7, 8, 9, 10 being output in day 1, 2, 3, 4, 5, 6, 7 leaving *date* with the value 11. The next 3 executions will produce the other dates leaving the inner loop with a value 32 in *date*. This will cause an exit since it is greater than the length of the month 31. You can trace for yourself what happens in the other extreme cases.

- *Satisfaction of program specifications*

  The program specifications are satisfied with perhaps a slight adjustment in the output format to line up the dates under the day names. Because strings are left justified and numbers right justified in their fields, you can adjust the format by including some blanks ahead of day one.

Problems

The problems marked with an asterisk are more mathematical.

Use the systematic method to solve these problems:

1.   Determine the number of quarters, dimes, nickels, and cents that must be given to a customer in change if the total amount of the change is less than one dollar. You are to give a minimum number of coins. (**Hint:** The operators **div** and **mod** may be useful.)

2.   Output a calendar for any year that you specify. You are to be given the year number, say 1995, and the day number on which the year begins. Watch out for leap years.

3.   How much should you pay for an annuity of $10,000 per year paid at the end of every year for 5 years if the trust company gives an interest rate of 8 percent a year. An annuity is an annual payment.

*4.   If when one integer is divided by another (smaller) integer there is no remainder the smaller integer is said to be an **exact divisor** of the first. Determine all the exact divisors of any integer between 1 and 100 on request. (**Hint:** The **mod** operator may be useful.)

*5.   A prime number is one that has no exact divisors except 1 and itself. Find all the prime numbers between 1 and 300, outputting them 5 to a line.

*6.   To find the individual digits in an integer we can use the **div** and **mod** operators. For example, if the integer consists of two digits, say 87 then from these:

$$87 \text{ mod } 10 = 7$$

and

$$87 \text{ div } 10 = 8$$

we can get the two digits. The problem is to find the digits of any integer that is supplied. The integer may consist of from 1 to 6 digits.

Questions for Discussion

1.   Sometimes programmers refer to statements in the programming language, such as Turing, as lines of code. Is code really an appropriate term to use?

2.   Sometimes programmers who are developing a program in a step-by-step way from the English language specification to the final program speak of the in-between sets as being written in pseudo-code. Is this a good term to use?

3.   Why does having a system for going about solving problems help you to be a better problem solver?

4.   Why do we not worry very much about the efficiency of the algorithms we use for solving many problems?

Technical Terms you should now know

known   correctness of program
unknown   efficiency of algorithm
intermediate value   exact divisor
algorithm   prime number
test data   annuity
tracing execution

Chapter 9

THE ELEMENTS OF PROGRAMMING: SELECTION

All programs can be constructed out of these three components: linear sequence, repetition, and selection constructs.

In the last chapter we looked at a systematic method for solving problems. The method led us systematically from a specification of the problem to be solved to a computer program to solve it.

The kinds of problems that we can attempt so far are limited by our knowledge of the basic elements of computer programming.

So far we have had only two of the basic constructs of all programs: the ·linear sequence of computer instructions and the repetition construct. There remains a third construct, namely **selection**, to complete our basic knowledge of programming.

All programs can be constructed out of these three components: linear sequence, repetition, and selection constructs.

Questions and Answers about Selection

Q.   Why should a program include selection constructs?

A.   So it can take different courses of action in different circumstances. Just the way you do.

Q.   When do you take different courses of action.

A.   When I wake up in the morning and look at the clock. If it is before 7 then I go back to sleep; if it is after 7 then I get up. (Maybe you have to get up earlier or later.)

Q.   What selection do you have?

A.   I select whether or not to go back to sleep. Ican spot a selection because there are keywords present.

Q.   What keywords?

A.   The words **if** and **then**. I say **if** it is before 7 **then** go back to sleep.

Q.   You then say "**if** it is after 7 **then** get up". Is that another selection?

A.   I suppose it is.

Q.   We could make it into a single selection by writing it this way

> **if** it is before 7 **then**
>   go back to sleep
> **else**
>   get up

then it looks very much like the selection construct of Turing?

A.   I never use the word "else".

Q.   Turing does. You see if it is *not* before 7 then it must be after 7 and you are wasting time repeating the same information. The part that comes between **if** and **then** is a **condition**. What is a condition?

A.   A condition is a statement that is either true or false. For example, "Denise is older than Sarah".

Q.   Does it matter which two friends you pick?

A.   No, it does not, but once I pick two names, the statement is either true or false. The phrase "is older than" describes a relationship between two people.

Q.   Are people always in the relationship?

A.   We can have relationships between integers, such as 10 is greater than 5.

Q.   We write that as

10 > 5

The sign > stands for "is greater than" and is called a **relational operator**,operator, relational or a comparison operator. Can you have the pair <>?

A.   No, it would say "is less than or is greater than" and that would always be true unless the two were equal. For example, 5 <> 6 is true, and so is 6<> 5. But 5 <> 5 is false.

Q.   Instead of <> we use **not=** as a relational operator. Is 5 **not**=5 true or false?

A.   False of course.

An Example of the Selection Construct

Here is a problem that requires the use of a selection construct:

Determine whether or not a person is old enough to apply for a driver's licence. We will assume that you must be at least 16 years old to apply.

We will follow our systematic method of problem solving.

• *What are knowns*? the age of the would-be applicant.

• *What is unknown*? whether or not the would-be applicant is old enough to apply.

- *Are there any intermediate values?* none.

- *Are there any constants?* the minimum age at which a person can apply.

- *What is the relationship between the known and unknown?* If we call the would-be applicant's age *age* and the minimum age *minAge* , then the relationship can be expressed this way:

```
if age >= minAge then
    the person is old enough to apply
else
    the person is not old enough to apply
```

- *How are results to be displayed?* The result, or actually what is unknown, will be output as a statement.

- *Devise the program.* Here is the complete program:

```
% The "driver" program
% Determines whether or not a person
% is old enough to apply for a driver's licence
var age: int
const minAge := 16
put "Enter your age"
get age
if age >= minAge then
    put "You are old enough to apply"
else
    put "You are not old enough to apply"
end if
```

The selection construct begins with the keyword **if** and ends with the keywords **end if**.

Here is the flowchart for this program.

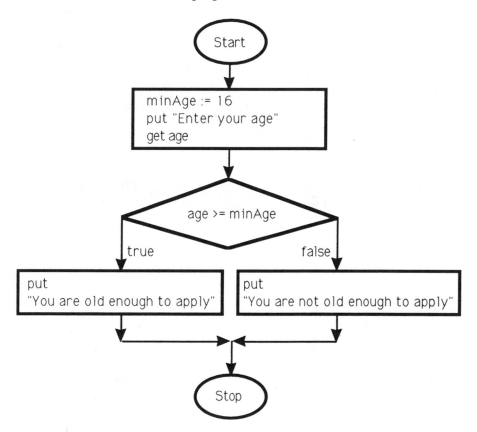

- *Run the program on test data.*
  Here is a sample execution window:

```
Enter your age
15
You are not old enough to apply
```

In this case, when *age=15,* the condition

age >= minAge

is false since *minAge* is 16. This means that the statement following the keyword **else** is executed. We should test the program on other ages say 19 and 16 to be sure it is giving reasonable results.

The statement (or statements) between the **then** and the **else** keywords are called the **then clause**. Those between the keywords **else** and **end if** are called the **else clause**. Which one of these two clauses is selected depends on whether the condition after the keyword **if** is true or false. This is called a two-way selection because there are two possible paths.

Problems

1. You are asked to find the highest mark in a series of marks that are to be provided by the user. Devise a program to do this. The marks can range from 0 to 100.

2. A class of students writes an exam that is marked out of 100. Write a program to find the range of marks, that is, the difference between the highest and lowest marks.

3. A special mark such as –1 is used to signify the end of a series of marks on input. You still can arrange to stop the program if an unsuitable mark is entered (negative other than –1, or greater than 100). If you do this, you should output an error message to the user. Write a program that does this where the purpose of the program is to calculate the number of *A*s (80 and over) and failures (less than 50) in the exam results of a class of students.

*4. You are asked to find the value of *x* between 0 and 1 that makes the function *f(x)* a minimum where

$$f(x) = 3x^2 - 2x + 1$$

Hint: compute values of *f(x)* for *x* going in steps of 0.1 from 0 to *x* and keep track of its smallest value and at what value of *x* this occurs.

Three-way Selection

Here the problem is: To divide a class of students into three with those having names beginning with A to F in group A, those from G to P in group B and those from Q to Z in group C. The students enter their names and are then told which group they are in.

We will not follow the systematic method but will move quickly to the final program.The knowns are the names of the students. The unknowns are the letters of the groups that they are in. Here is a program that will work for a series of students.

```
% The "split" program
% Splits a group of students into
% three classes A, B, and C
const endA := "F"
const endB := "P"
var name : string
const endName := "zzz"
loop
    put "Enter last name"
    get name
    exit when name = "zzz"
    if name <= endA then
        put "You are in group A"
    elsif name <= endB then
        put "You are in group B"
    else
        put "You are in group C"
    end if
end loop
```

Here the selection construct has the keyword **elsif** followed by the condition *name <= endB*. If the *name <= endA* the student is placed in group A and the program's control goes directly to the instruction following the **end if**. If the **elsif** condition is tested the name will be greater than *endA*. These students between *endA* and *endB* will be in group B. The **else** clause deals with all the rest who must have names greater than *endB*.

This program should be tested for students in each group and those near the borderline. Here is a sample test execution:

```
Enter last name
Chu
You are in group A
Enter last name
Lahti
Your are in group B
Enter last name
Polowski
You are in group C
Enter last name
zzz
```

This test showed that the boundaries are not correct if we want any names beginning with "P" to be in group B. We will have to change *endB* to "Q". Similarly *endA* should be "G". Testing can eliminate mistakes but it cannot prove that a program is correct. We should make the changes and test again.

An **if...then...else..end if** construct with **elsif** is called a **cascaded selection**. You can have as many **elsif**s as you need so that you can produce selections that are four-way, five-way, and so on.

Here is the flowchart for this program.

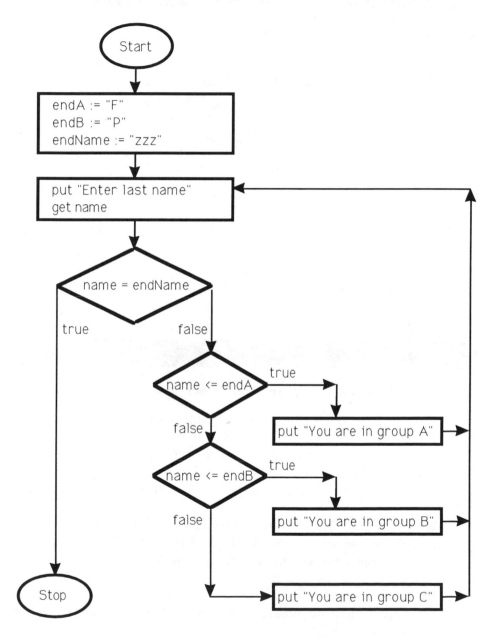

Errors that you might make

- Forgetting the **end if** in an **if...then** selection construct.

- Confusing which part of a selection is executed when the condition after the **if** is true: the **then** clause or the **else** clause.

- Adding extra **end if**s when there are **elsif**s.

- Spelling **elsif** as two words, namely **else if**.

- Forgetting to put a condition after any **elsif**.

- Putting a condition after an **else**.

- Using < in a condition when <= is the correct comparison operator.

- Using =< rather than >=.

- Forgetting to test all alternatives in a selection.

Problems

The problems marked with an asterisk are more mathematical.

1.   You are to determine the amount of postage to be put on a letter given its weight in grams. Up to 30g, the stamp required is 48¢, then up to 50g is 70¢, up to 100g is 90¢. The rate is constant after that being 18¢ for each 50g or less. Make sure to use constants for the various rates as the post office is always raising the values and you want to be able to change them easily.

2.   Write a program that asks a person for their age and outputs which type of movie ticket is appropriate. There are four classes child, student, adult, and senior. Choose appropriate constants for the age breaks.

3.   A meal is taxed at 7% if the cost is greater than $4.00. Write a program to read a series of costs and output the total for each meal. You are to enter a negative cost to stop the repetition.

4.   Federal income tax is to be calculated in stages on taxable income. On the first $27,500 you pay 17% tax, on the next $27,500 you pay 24%, and on the rest 29%. Write a program to read in a taxable income and compute the federal tax to the nearest cent.

5.   A list of names is input in alphabetic order. There are some duplicates in the list. Arrange to output the list with the duplicate names omitted. This is useful for a mailing program where you do not want to send two letters to the same person. Assume the names are just last names.

*6.   Write a program to determine how many digits there are in a real number to the left of the decimal point.

Hint: when you divide a real number by 10 the number of digits to the left of the decimal point decreases by one.

*7.   A **quadratic equation** is one with the form

$$ax^2 + bx + c = 0$$

where a, b and c are real numbers. The values of x for which this equation is satisfied are called its **roots**. There is a simple formula for the values of the roots. In the formula the quantity

$$b^2 - 4a\ c$$

discriminates between the three possible situations. It is called the **discriminant** of the equation. There are three possible situations

    1. If the discriminant is positive there are two real roots.
    2. If the discriminant is zero the two real roots are equal.
    3. If the discriminant is negative there are no real roots.

Write a program to input values for a, b, and c for a quadratic equation and output the nature of its roots.

Nested Selections

Here is the problem: Determine the size of bathing suit a person should wear. There are four sizes to choose from depending on your weight

size	*Range of weight*
small :	minSmall - maxSmall
medium :	minMedium - maxMedium
large :	minLarge - maxLarge
xlarge :	minXLarge - maxXLarge

There are only five different constants here since

maxSmall = minMedium
maxMedium = MinLarge
maxLarge = MinXLarge

We will not specify what these five constant values actually are but can fill them in as required. The values would be different for men and women and would depend on whether the weights were given in pounds or kilograms.

```
% The "bathing" program
% Determines the size of bathing suit you need
const minSmall := (...you fill in...)
const minMedium := (...you fill in...)
const minLarge := (...you fill in...)
const minXLarge := (...you fill in...)
const maxXLarge := (...you fill in...)
var weight : int
put "Please enter your weight"
get weight
```

```
if weight >= minSmall and
    weight <= maxXLarge then
    if weight < minMedium then
        put "size small"
    elsif weight < minLarge then
        put "size medium"
    elsif weight < minXLarge then
        put "size large"
    else
        put "size xlarge"
    end if
else
    put "Sorry we cannot fit you"
end if
```

Here there are two selection constructs nested one inside the other. The outer one is a two-way selection which selects between persons who can be fitted with a bathing suit and those who cannot. For those who can be fitted there is a second four-way selection nested in the **then** clause of the outer selection construct. This inner selection decides which of the four sizes a person who can be fitted should wear. This inner construct is a cascaded **if**; it has two **elsif**s.

Here is the flowchart for the program.

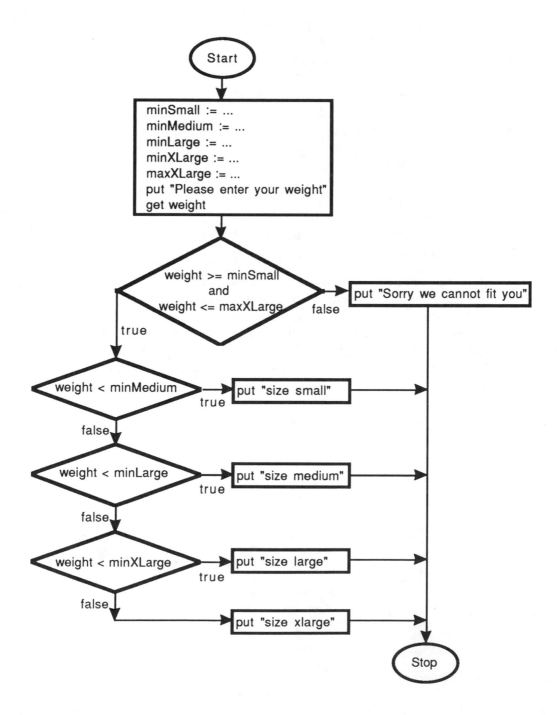

Another Method for Multi-way Selections

We have seen that a cascaded **if** can be used to select one out of many possible alternatives. There is another kind of multi-way selection that is perhaps simpler when the different choices to be made depend on an integer. This uses the **case construct**.

Here is an example problem using **case**. A user of a program is asked to select one of a number of alternatives from a menu. The different alternatives in the menu are numbered so the selection is made by entering the number of the alternative the user wants. For example, here is a menu listing choices of breakfast specials:

```
1 – juice, muffin, coffee
2 – cereal, toast, milk
3 – egg, toast, coffee
4 – banana, granola, milk
5 – grapefruit, bacon, eggs, coffee
```

Here is a program that displays the menu and, after asking the user which choice is to be served, gives the cost. If the price of the meal is over $4.00 a tax of 7% is to be paid.

```
% The "breakfast" program
% Presents a menu, asks for a selection
% then outputs the cost including tax if
% cost is greater than$4.00
% Display menu for user
put "1 – juice, muffin, coffee"
put "2 – cereal, toast, milk"
put "3 – egg, toast, coffee"
put "4 – banana, granola, milk"
put "5 – grapefruit, bacon, egg, coffee"
put ""
put "Please indicate your choice by number"
var choice: int
get choice
var cost, tax: real
case choice of
```

```
        label 1: cost := 2.50
        label 2: cost := 2.50
        label 3: cost := 3.00
        label 4: cost := 3.50
        label 5: cost := 5.00
        label: put "You must enter an integer between",
                    "1 and 5"
    end case
    if cost <= 4.00 then
        put "Please pay", cost : 8 : 2
    else
        tax := round (cost * 7) / 100
        put "Please pay", cost : 8 : 2, " plus ", tax,
                " tax, total is ",  cost + tax
    end if
```

In the **case** construct if *choice* is 1 then **label** 1 is selected and *cost* is set to 2.50. Since the cost of selection 2 is the same as for selection 1, we could have had a single line in the **case** construct

```
        label 1, 2 : cost := 2.50
```

which is selected for choice 1 and choice 2.

The last **label** of the **case** has no choice number. This alternative is selected if the user accidentally presses 6 or 9 say. A reminder is given that only integers between 1 and 5 are valid choices. This clause of the **case** construct is called the **otherwise clause**; it covers all the possibilities that are not valid. If the user enters a string or a real number by mistake, the **get** *choice* instruction will fail since *choice* is defined as an integer variable. This stops program execution with an error message.

Here is the flowchart for the case statement in this program.

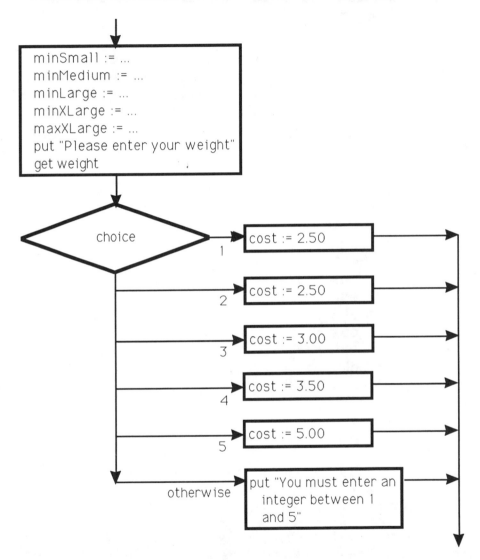

After the **case** construct (ending with **end case**) there is a two-way selection of the normal **if**...**then**...**else**... **end if** construction.

User-Friendly Programs

Programs that display menus and have prompts are easier for users to use. We have tried to make all our programs so far user-friendly in this sense. Another way to make them user-friendly is to make them "forgiving" when a user enters an inappropriate choice and allow the user to try again. We could make our *breakfast* program forgiving by changing the part containing the **case** construct to this

```
loop
    case choice of
        label 1,2 :
            cost := 2.50
            exit
        label 3 :
            cost := 3.00
            exit
        label 4 :
            cost := 3.50
            exit
        label 5 :
            cost := 5.00
            exit
        label :
            put "You must enter an ",
                "integer between 1 and 5"
            put "Try again"
    end case
end loop
```

Each one of the valid choices has an **exit** in its selection clause except the otherwise clause. This causes the program to leave the loop except when the user has entered an inappropriate integer.

Notice that each clause of a **case** selection may contain any number of instructions.

Errors that you might make

- Not having two **end if**s if you are using one **if** nested inside another.

- Forgetting the **end case** in a case construct.

- Trying to use values for labels in a case that are not integers.

- Forgetting to declare the variable whose name appears before the **of** in a **case** statement.

- Forgetting the **of** in a **case**.

- Forgetting the comma between two integers after the keyword **label**.

- Leaving out the otherwise clause of a **case** construct when it would be friendlier to the user to be told that the data input is wrong

Problems

1.   Devise a program to display a multiple choice exam question about selection and make comments about the various answers to the person who answers the question. There should be five choices of answers every one of which sounds plausible. Make it forgiving if the person answering chooses an inappropriate number.

2.   Devise a fun program that offers a menu of five different possible choices each one of which requires the user to enter some data before the computer responds. Have the program arranged to be played again and again until the option of stopping is chosen by the user.

Hint: a possible option might be to say how old a person is. You would request the year of birth to be entered.

3.   A test is marked out of 10. Letter grades are assigned on the basis of the mark: Grade A is 8, 9, 10, Grade B is 7, Grade C is 6, Grade D is 5, Grade F is any mark less than these. Write a program to convert a series of test marks to letter grades. To stop the program enter a grade that is larger than 10. Can your program be forgiving?

Questions for Discussion

1.   One of the great advances in computer programming came when it was recognized that all programs could be constructed out of the three basic constructs: linear sequence, repetition, and selection. Does that mean that all programs are necessarily constructed that way?

2.   What is the value of having an **elsif** in the Turing language? Could you get along without it?

3.   Why is it important to try to make computer programs user friendly?

4.   Why must commercial software be "forgiving" with its users?

Technical Terms you should now know

selection   multi-way selection
if ... then ... else ... end if   nested selections
then clause   case construct
else clause   **case**
relational operator   **label**
three-way selection   user-friendly program
elsif   otherwise clause
cascaded selection   forgiving program

Chapter 10

DIVIDE AND CONQUER: SUBPROGRAMS

United we stand,
divided we fall.

When we are attempting to solve a problem one of the first things we can do is to see if it can be broken down into smaller problems.

The problem as a whole may seem difficult but each individual subproblem may be relatively easy to solve.

Sometimes the individual subproblems have already been solved and we can just use the solutions we already have.

In this chapter we will see how to create subprograms to solve subproblems and how to put them together to solve the larger problem.

This technique is often referred to by the ancient strategy used to win wars: "Divide and conquer". And the sensible counter strategy "United we stand, divided we fall".

If we hope to reuse a subprogram created for one problem in another problem, we must be careful that it is written in a particular way.

To create such a versatile subprogram, we must completely describe the variables that carry information from the main program into the subprogram and those that carry information out.

Questions and Answers about Subprograms

Q. Why should programs be broken into subprograms?

A. Because small problems are easier to solve than bigger problems.

Q. How can you tell whether or not a problem can be broken into subproblems?

A. A problem can be broken down when it is a larger problem with a number of separable pieces.

Q. Could you give me an example of such a problem?

A. One example might be to find the median exam mark in a class of students.

Q. What is the median mark?

A. It is the mark that divides the class in two; half of the students have a mark above the median, half below.

Q. Is it the same as the average mark?

A. No, the average does not necessarily divide the class into two halves. For example, more than half may be above the average.

Q. You know how to get the average by dividing the total of all the marks by the number of students in the class. How do you get the median?

A. That's the problem.

Q. Can you think of a way?

A. Arrange the class in order of ascending (or descending) marks and look for the half-way point?

Q. That's a great suggestion. Does that break up the problem into subproblems?

A. I see two subproblems, one to arrange the class in order, the other is to look for the half-way point to find the median.

Q. Arranging a list in order is called sorting the list. First you sort, then you look for the half-way point. How does that help?

A.   I only have to concentrate on one thing at a time. It's simpler.

Q.   And, you may already have solved the sorting problem and can just reuse an old subprogram to do the job. It's like remembering the answer.

A.   Should I save all my subprograms in case they may be used again?

Q.   A lot of subprograms are only useful in the particular problem for which they were designed but we should be on the lookout for opportunities to create subprograms that have more general use.

A.   Could any subprogram be used generally?

Q.   Yes provided you were careful not to couple the subprogram too closely to the particular problem it was created for.

A.   Is there a library of generally useful subprograms?

Q.   There certainly is. We say they are predefined in the Turing language.

Types of Subprograms

In Turing there are two kinds of subprograms called **functions** and **procedures**. A function has a value. A procedure does something.

Perhaps the best way to appreciate the difference between these two subprogram types is to examine the ones that have already been constructed for you to use as part of the Turing language. These are the **predefined subproprams**. We have already used a lot of predefined functions. Having these available saves us the trouble of solving part of our problem; we just use someone else's solution. Usually we do not see the instructions in the predefined subprograms. We just have to know what information we must provide and what information or action is produced by the subprogram. The subprogram keeps the workings hidden from us. It is sometimes said to act like a "black box". We see what it does but we do not see how it does it.

This characteristic of hiding information is often helpful so we do not get overwhelmed by details when we are trying to see how a program works.

Predefined Functions

Most of the predefined subprograms in Turing are functions. We have been using a large number of them already. For example, the *sqrt* function. If we write the program

put sqrt (9)

we are using *sqrt.* The item that appears in parentheses after the name of the function is called the parameter of the function. This parameter must be of the data type **real** or **int** It can be a constant as it is here or it may be a variable, or an expression. For example, we could have this program where a variable is the parameter:

var number: **real** := 9
put sqrt (number)

which would give the same output namely 3. Or we could have this where an arithmetic expression is the parameter:

put sqrt (2 / 5)

If we try to give a parameter which is negative, it will not work because   the square root of a negative number is not defined.

In all cases the value produced by the function is a real number (although it may be output as an integer).

Here is an example of a predefined function that has more than one parameter: the *repeat* function.

The output produced by

put repeat ("*", 5)

is *****. Of the two parameters separated by a comma, the first is the pattern to be repeated and must be of data type **string**. The second parameter is the number of repetitions and must be of data type **int** The function itself has a data type which is **string**. We will now create a function of our own which does exactly the same thing.

Defining a Function

We will call our function *again*. We want it to produce the same kind of value as *repeat* so that if we write

put again ("*", 5)

we would get the output *****. Here is the definition of *again*:

```
function again (pattern: string, howMany: int) : string
    var value: string := ""
    for i: 1 .. howMany
        value := value + pattern
    end for
    result value
end again
```

This diagram illustrates formal parameters, actual parameters, local variables and the results of the again function.

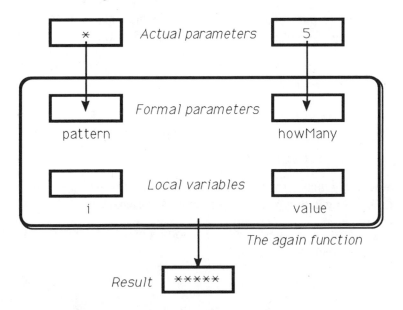

- The definition begins with the keyword **function**, followed by the name of the function, then, in parentheses, the list of parameters each giving its own data type, then, after the closing parentheses, a colon and the data type of the function's value.

- The body of the function contains the set of instructions for producing the value to be returned by that function. The function ends with the keyword **result** followed by that value.

- The variable *value* is declared as a string and initialized to the null string in the first line of the body of the function. We say *value* is a variable that is local to the function, a **local variable**. The actual result is created by the counted loop.

- The parameters in the function definition are called **formal parameters**. They give the form that the **actual parameters** must take. They also give their data types.

- The formal parameters are variable names. The actual parameters given when the function is used, can be variable names, expressions or constants.

- If the actual parameters are variable names they can have the same names as the formal parameters, but usually don't.

- If the program contains the definition of a function, the function must be defined before it is used.

- The sequence of parameters is important. For example if we had defined the function *again* and then had this instruction in the program

  put again (5, "*")

  we would get an error message telling us that the actual parameters were of the wrong data type. We have them in the wrong order.

- There must be a one-to-one correspondence between the formal and actual parameters.

- The formal parameters must be variables, the actual parameters need not be as long as their data type matches the data type of the formal parameter variable.

Another very useful predefined function is *index*. When it is called by an instruction of this form

put index (s, pattern)

it outputs the position of the string *pattern* in the string *s*. If there is no occurrence of *pattern* in *s*then it outputs a zero. If it occurs more than once, the leftmost occurrence is given. For example

put index ("Canada", "a")

would produce a value 2 the position of the first *a* in *Canada*.

Errors that you might make

- Forgetting to include the data types of the parameters in a function definition.

- Forgetting to follow the list of formal parameters in parentheses by a colon then the data type of the function's value.

- Forgetting to include the keyword **result** followed by the function's value.

- Using **end function** instead of **end** followed by the function's name.

- Getting the actual parameters of a function in the wrong order.

- Forgetting to define the function before it is used.

Problems

1.   Write a function subprogram called *square* that will have a value that is the square of the value of its parameter. Include it in a main program that has this instruction

put "The square of 5 is", square (5)

The output should be

The square of 5 is 25

2.   Write a function subprogram called *find* that will do what the predefined function *index* does. Use it in a program to eliminate the vowels in a word that is read into the computer.

3.   Use the predefined function *index* or the *find* function you created for question 2 in another function called *howOften* , which will count the number of occurrences of a pattern in a string. For example,

put howOften ("Canada", "a")

will produce the result 3, the number of times that *a* occurs in *Canada*.

Note: In a program, when one function uses another, the definition of the used function must precede the definition of the function that uses it.

4.   Write a function subprogram that determines for any date the number of days that have elapsed since the first of the year for that date. (Include the day itself.) Use the function in a program to determine the time elapsed between any two dates in the same year.

*5.   In a right-angled triangle the square of the hypotenuse is equal to the sum of the squares of the other two sides. Use the function *square* that you created for question 1 and the predefined function *sqrt* to find the length of the hypotenuse of any right-angled triangle whose two other sides are input.

Predefined Procedures

A function has a value, a procedure does something. One predefined procedure that we have met so far is *locate*. It is used in the form

locate (row, column)

For example, if we use these instructions in the program

locate (10, 20)
put "*", ..

an asterisk will be output in row 10, column 20 on the screen. Remember for the PC there are 25 rows and 80 columns on the screen. The *locate* procedure places the cursor at the specified position. The **put** instruction outputs the asterisk there. The predefined procedure *locate* has two parameters, the row number and the column number. They must be in that order, first the row then the column.

Here is a predefined procedure with only one parameter

colorback (colorNumber)

where for character graphics on the PC the parameter *colorNumber* can be a number between 0 and 7 inclusive. It changes the color of the background. The procedure *color* (*colorNumber*) changes the color of what characters are displayed.

cls is a predefined procedure with no parameters. It clears the screen and changes it to the current background color.

There are many predefined procedures for drawing pixel graphics but we will look at them later.

Defining a Procedure

To show you how they work, we will write a procedure called *greet* that greets you by outputting *Hello* followed by your name. Here is its definition:

```
procedure greet (person : string)
    put "Hello ", person
end greet
```

This procedure has one parameter which is of data type string. A procedure has no value so we do not give a data type for it as we did for a function. The keyword **procedure** is followed by the procedure's name then, in parentheses, the names and data types of its parameters. Here, there is only one parameter, *person,* and it is of data type **string**. The body of the procedure is only one instruction.

Here is a program that uses this procedure:

```
(place definition of greet here)
var name: string
put "Enter your name"
get name
greet (name)
```

The actual parameter *name* is in correspondence with the formal parameter *person*. These two identifiers could be the same but do not have to be.

Variable Parameters in Procedures

Whenever a procedure changes the value of one of its parameters, that parameter must be indicated as a **variable parameter** by having its name in the parameter list preceded by the keyword **var**.

Here is a procedure that changes a word so that its letters are in the reverse order.

```
procedure reverse (var word : string)
    var newWord: string := ""
    for decreasing count : length (word) .. 1
        newWord := newWord + word (count)
    end for
    word := newWord
end reverse
```

Here is a program that uses *reverse*.

```
(definition of procedure reverse)
var name: string
put "Enter a series of names, end with stop"
loop
    get name
    exit when name = "stop"
    reverse (name)
    put name
end loop
```

This diagram illustrates the formal parameter (name with the value "Alice"), actual parameter and local variables used for the *reverse* procedure. After the procedure is finished executing, the value of name will have been reversed to "ecilA".

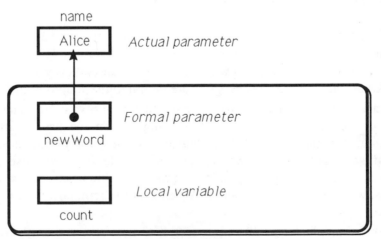

name

Alice   *Actual parameter*

              Formal parameter

newWord

              Local variable

count

The reverse procedure

Notice that the actual parameter of the procedure is a variable. You could not write

reverse ("John")

because there would be no variable in which you could place the reversed name. The actual parameters of all variable parameters must themselves be variables. When a parameter is not a variable parameter, the actual parameter may be a variable but it can be a constant. It must, however, have the right data type.

The parameters of a procedure show the information that is being passed into the procedure, or the information that is being passed out of the procedure back to the main program. Whenever information is passed out, the parameter must be a variable parameter. A function does not pass information out except by having a value. This means that a function never has any variable parameters. We say that a function cannot have **side effects**; it simply returns a value.

Global Variables

We have seen that the names of the formal parameters and the actual parameters need not be the same, although we can, if we like, use the same names.

When we do use exactly the same names, we can actually get along without any parameters at all. This is because the values of all variables declared in the main program are accessible to the subprogram. We say variables declared in the main program are **global** to the subprogram.

In a way this is a dangerous thing because it allows us to change the value of a global variable without warning. When we use parameters, remember, any parameter that is changed by the subprogram is clearly labelled **var**. That is why we say the safest rule is "never use global variables". It is not good programming practice. Sometimes, if just out of laziness, we do use global variables. When we use them, however, we must do so carefully.

In this example, the problem is to read in three names and output them in alphabetic order.

First, we give the program that does not use any global variables.

```
% The "trio" program
% Reads three names and outputs
% them in alphabetic order
var name1, name2, name3: string

procedure readin (var name1, name2, name3: string)
    % Read in three names
    put "Enter first name: " ..
    get name1
    put "Enter second name: " ..
    get name2
    put "Enter third name: " ..
    get name3
end readin

procedure order (var name1, name2, name3: string)
    % Sorts three names into alphabetic order
    var temp: string
    if name2 < name1 then
        % interchange them
        temp := name2
        name2 := name1
        name1 := temp
    end if
    if name3 < name2 then
        % interchange them
        temp := name3
        name3 := name2
        name2 := temp
    end if
    % Must still test to see if name2 < name1
    if name2 < name1 then
        % interchange them
        temp := name2
        name2 := name1
        name1 := temp
    end if
end order
```

```
procedure output (name1, name2, name3: string)
    % Output names in alphabetic order
    put "The names in alphabetic order are"
    put name1
    put name2
    put name3
end output

readin (name1, name2, name3)
order (name1, name2, name3)
output (name1, name2, name3)
```

To get the program that uses global variables, we can simply remove the parentheses and what they contain in the definitions of the three procedures and in the three statements of the main program that use the procedures. We can only do this because we used the same variable names for the actual and formal parameters.

In fact, the program would work in the same way if we did not break it into three procedures. Simply remove the lines that enclose the bodies of the procedures, the ones beginning with the keyword **procedure** and the ones with the concluding **end**. As well, we would remove the last three lines. Here is the same program without procedures.

```
% The "three" program
% Reads three names and outputs
% them in alphabetic order
var name1, name2, name3: string
put "Enter first name: " ..
get name1
put "Enter second name: " ..
get name2
put "Enter third name: " ..
get name3

% Sorts three names into alphabetic order
var temp: string

if name2 < name1 then
    % interchange them
    temp := name2
```

```
            name2 := name1
            name1 := temp
        end if
        if name3 < name2 then
            % interchange them
            temp := name3
            name3 := name2
            name2 := temp
        end if
        % Must still test to see if name2 < name1
        if name2 < name1 then
            % interchange them
            temp := name2
            name2 := name1
            name1 := temp
        end if

        % Output names in alphabetic order
        put "The names in alphabetic order are"
        put name1
        put name2
        put name3
```

Sometimes people simply take a program like this and saw it up into subprograms using global variables.

Versatility and Independence of Subprograms

If we want to use a subprogram created for one program in another program, then we must not use global variables. The main purpose of having predefined subprograms, either of your own creation or ones built into the Turing language, is that you do not need to read them to find out what variables they change. You only need to see the list of formal parameters with their data types.

For example, we could use our *order* procedure to arrange three strings in alphabetic order.

Errors that you might make

- Using **end procedure** instead of **end** followed by the procedure's name.

- Forgetting to use the keyword **var** before a variable parameter in the list of a procedure's formal parameters.

- Forgetting that any parameter that is altered by a procedure must be a variable parameter.

- Using a constant actual parameter for a variable parameter.

- Not including the definition of a procedure before it is used.

- Having a variable parameter in a function.

- Using global variables when you could use parameters in procedures.

- Forgetting to declare local variables in a procedure.

Problems

1.   Write a procedure called *label* that will print an address label. The five parameters will be name, street, town or city, province or state, and postal code.

2.   Write a procedure called *readinfo* that will read in the information necessary to produce an address label as in question 1.

3.   Combine the procedures *label* and *readinfo* of question 1 and 2 in a program to read data and output labels.

4.   Write a procedure that will draw a box of asterisks on the screen. Have as parameters: the length and width of the box in character spaces, the row and column where the upper-left corner of the box is to be located, and the color of the asterisks. Test the procedure by asking the user to input values for the parameters and drawing the required box.

5.   Write a procedure to draw a solid right-angled triangle of asterisks and use the procedure to draw a row of such triangles on the screen. The sides bordering the right angle of the triangles will be parallel to the edges of the screen.

Questions for Discussion

In these situations, how might you break the problem into subproblems? Do not write any programs.

1.   Two classes write the same exam and you are to find the median mark for each class and then for the two classes as a whole.

2.   How would you go about having the computer create two, more or less, equal baseball teams from a number of people? Are there subprograms here?

3.   How would you read a series of words and output them in lines of maximum length 60 characters?

4.   Could you use a function instead of the procedure *reverse* described in this chapter?

Technical Terms you should now know

median   local variable
average   formal parameter
sorting   actual parameter
function   variable parameter
procedure   side effect
predefined subprogram   global variable

Chapter 11

PIXEL GRAPHICS

. . . by placing these dots on the screen
we can build up
very complex pictures.

We have seen how to place characters on the screen in any position we want. In this way we can build up a picture on the screen.

Characters can be displayed in color and the background could also be colored.

You can also draw pictures by placing pixels on the screen. A pixel is just a dot and is much smaller than a character. But by placing these dots carefully on the screen, you can build up very complex pictures.

In this way you can produce detailed graphics.

Questions and Answers about Graphics Subprograms

Q.   When you locate the cursor ready to output a character what instruction do you use?

A.   You use a *locate* instruction like this

locate (10, 20)

Q.   What are the numbers in parentheses?

A.   The 10 is the row number and the 20 the column number. There are 25 possible rows and 80 possible columns on the screen.

Q.   Where do you start the row count (or the column count)?

A.   At the top-left corner of the screen, that is the **origin** of the counting.

Q.   Does this *locate* instruction remind you of anything?

A.   It looks like the call to a predefined procedure called *locate*.

Q.   And what are the numbers in parentheses?

A.   They are the actual parameters.

Q.   How do we get the character that we output to be in color, say red?

A.   By using the instruction

color (4)

I suppose color is another predefined procedure.

Q.   How do you know red is 4?

A.   I looked it up in Appendix 4.

Q.   In pixel graphics we use a single instruction to locate, specify the color, and output the pixel. It is of this form

drawdot (x, y, c)

What are *x*, *y*, and *c*?

A.   They must give the location and the color number.

Q.   What are *x* and *y*?

A.   They are the **coordinates** of the point on the screen where the pixel will be drawn.

Q.   What is x?

A.   It must be the distance horizontally to the point from the left side.

Q.   And what is y?

A.   It might be the distance vertically to the point, from the top of the screen, I guess.

Q.   No it is from the bottom. The origin (or starting point of the coordinates for pixel graphics) is at the lower left of the screen.

A.   We've already met coordinates like this in graph plotting. Or Math.

Q.   What is the scale of plotting? How many pixel positions are possible?

A.   I don't know.

Q.   It depends on the graphics system you have on your computer but a very common one, called VGA, has 320 horizontal positions and 480 vertical positions. How many total possible positions would that be?

A.   It would be $320 \times 480 = 153{,}600$ possible positions for a pixel. If you made a picture up out of pixels you would hardly be able to see each separate pixel.

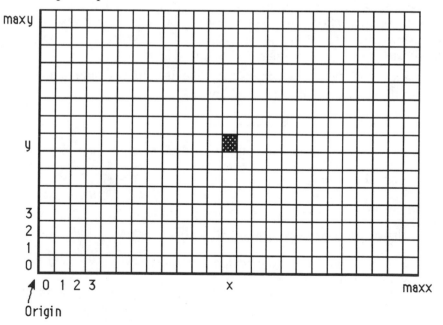

Drawing Lines and Boxes

Plotting pictures pixel by pixel is very slow, so usually pictures are made by drawing lines or curves and then coloring in closed figures. To draw a line you use an instruction in this form:

drawline (x1, y1, x2, y2, c)

Here the line is between two points whose coordinates are *(x1, y1)* and *(x2, y2)* and the color number is *c*.

You can find out how big the screen is in pixels by using the predefined functions *maxx* and *maxy*. The *x*-coordinate can be any integer between 0 and *maxx*, Similarly *y* can be any integer between 0 and *maxy*. If you specify a point off the screen, then that part off the screen is omitted.

Here is an instruction that draws a red line diagonally from the upper-left corner of the screen, to the lower-right corner.

drawline (0, maxy, maxx, 0, 4)

We should really use this declaration

const red := 4

then the instruction can be

drawline (0, maxy, maxx, 0, red)

You can draw a blue colored box with 4 lines in this way. We want the box to fill the lower-left quarter of the screen.

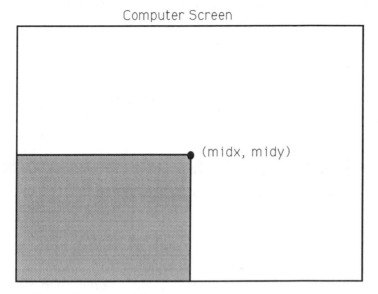

Here is the program:

```
% The "quarter" program
% Fills the lower-left quarter
% of the screen with blue
% Find the coordinates of the mid-point
% These must be integers
const midx := round (maxx / 2)
const midy := round (maxy / 2)
const blue := 1
drawline (0, 0, midx, 0, blue)
drawline (0, 0, 0, midy, blue)
drawline (0, midy, midx, midy, blue)
drawline (midx, 0, midx, midy, blue)
drawfill (1, 1, blue, blue)
```

In this program we use the instruction that fills a closed outline with color. It has the form:

drawfill (xinside, yinside, fillcolor, bordercolor)

The point (*xinside, yinside*) is any point inside the closed border.

We can draw a box with a single *drawbox* instruction instead of four *drawline* instructions. For our example it would be

> drawbox (0, 0, midx, midy, blue)

The two points given as parameters are the lower-left and the upper-right corners of the box.

Holding Graphics on the Screen

Whenever a program finishes executing, an indication appears to warn the user that the program is finished. When windows are being used, as with the Macintosh, this warning appears in the window heading and does not interfere with the output. But for the PC, there is a prompt indicating what to do next. This prompt can spoil the look of a graphic that is taking up the whole screen. To prevent this, all programs could place these two instructions at their end.

> **var** reply: **string** (1)
> getch (reply)

The *getch* is a predefined procedure that expects one character to be input, until you press a character, for example the space bar, nothing will happen. When you do press a character, the end of execution prompt will appear.

You could have a parameterless procedure *hold* defined in this way

> **procedure** hold
>   **var** reply: **string** (1)
>   getch (reply)
> **end** hold

Then in the main program you could just use the instruction *hold* at the end. The *hold* procedure might be included anywhere in a program to stop execution so you could assess what has been done so far. You start execution again by pressing the space bar.

Solving a Graphics Problem

Here is the problem:

Write a program to draw a checkerboard pattern of blue and red squares on the screen. It should have 6 squares across and 4 squares up. The lower-left square is to be red.

Computer Screen

Red   Blue

We will use the divide and conquer method of solving this problem. We have several subproblems here:

• To find the proper size of the squares.

• To find the coordinates of the corners of the squares.

• To be able to draw a colored square of any size at any corner.

• To be able to draw the two kinds of rows of squares required to make a checkerboard.

We will begin with the first subproblem: To find the size of the squares which must be an integer.

The size d in pixels must be either *maxx* **div** 6 or *maxy* **div** 4 whichever is smaller. For the VGA graphics system we would find that *maxx* **div** 6 is 79 since *maxx* = 479 and *maxy* **div** 4 is also 79 since *maxy* = 319. The 4×6 pattern of squares fits the screen very well. We would write the program as a function this way:

```
function gridscale: int
    if maxx div 6 < maxy div 4 then
        result  maxx div 6
    else
        result maxy div 4
    end if
end gridscale
```

This will work for any graphics system. There are no parameters of *gridscale*, its value is the size of squares that allows a 4×6 pattern of squares on the screen. We refer to the value of *gridscale* as d.

Next the coordinates of the corners. They are at gridpoints. If we use the origin as the lower-left corner of the grid, then the x-coordinates will be

$$0, 0 + d, 0 + 2d, 0 + 3d, 0 + 4d, 0 + 5d, 0 + 6d$$

The y-coordinates will be

$$0, 0 + d, 0 + 2d, 0 + 3d, 0 + 4d$$

The central point will have coordinates

$$(3d, 2d)$$

We see we can refer to any grid point we like and do not have to create a special subprogram.

Next we need to create a subprogram to draw a square block of any size, color, and lower-left corner. Here is such a procedure

```
procedure drawblock (xll, yll, size, Color: int)
    drawbox (xll, yll, xll + size, yll + size, maxcolour)
    drawfill (xll + 2, yll + 2, Color, maxcolour)
end drawblock
```

Notice that we used Color as a formal parameter with a capital C. The word *color* is the name of a predefined procedure and is thus **reserved**. Turing, remember, distinguishes between upper and lower case letters.

We want now to produce two subprograms for drawing the two kinds of rows of squares for the checkerboard. We will call the one where the first square is in the specified color the even row, and call the procedure *drawevenrow*. Here is its definition:

```
procedure drawevenrow (row, Color: int)
    const d := gridscale
    for count: 0 .. 3
        drawblock (0 + 2 * count * d, row, d, Color)
    end for
end drawevenrow
```

And also the other one *drawoddrow:*

```
procedure drawoddrow (row, Color: int)
    const d := gridscale
    for count: 0 .. 3
        drawblock (d + 2 * count * d, row, d, Color)
    end for
end drawoddrow
```

Here now is the procedure that draws the checkerboard called *drawcheckers*. It uses all the other procedures.

```
procedure drawcheckers
    const d := gridscale
    % Draw red squares of checkerboard
    const red := 4
    for count: 0 .. 1
        drawevenrow (0 + 2 * count * d, red)
        drawoddrow (d + 2 * count * d, red)
    end for
    % Draw blue squares of checkerboard
    const blue := 1
    for count: 0 .. 1
        drawoddrow (0 + 2 * count * d, blue)
```

```
          drawevenrow (d + 2 * count * d, blue)
   end for
end drawcheckers
```

The problem is then solved by the program:

```
(copy function gridscale here)
(copy procedure drawblock here)
(copy procedure drawevenrow here)
(copy procedure drawoddrow here)
(copy procedure drawcheckers here)
% Here is the main program
drawcheckers
```

You will find that some of these programs can be used again.

Errors that you might make

- Using the upper-left corner of the screen as the origin rather than the lower-left corner.

- Assuming that all screens have the same number of pixels.

- Reversing the x and y in expressing coordinates.

- Forgetting to create an integer value for a pixel coordinate: writing *maxx* / 2 rather than *maxx* **div** 2.

- Not using the coordinates of a point inside a closed outline for *drawfill*.

- Trying to use the reserved word *color* as the name of a constant or variable.

Problems

1.   Modify the *drawcheckers* program so that it refers to two parameters, the two colors to be used. Use it in a program to draw a checkerboard with yellow and green squares instead of red and blue. Try other combinations.

2.   Write a procedure called drawtriangle which when used in this form

drawtriangle (xl, yl, base, height, Color)

will produce an **isosceles** triangle of given base and height, with its lower-left **vertex** at point (*xl, yl*). Use the procedure to draw such a blue triangle in every square of the grid. Use the function *gridscale* if you like.

3.   What happens if you use a negative value for either or both of the *base* and *height* in your *drawtriangle* procedure? Test it.

Drawing Closed Curves

In Turing there is a predefined procedure for drawing an oval. It has this form

drawoval (x, y, xRadius, yRadius, Color)

The oval has its center at (*x, y*). Its half-height is *yRadius* and its half-width is *xRadius*. To draw a circle, these two radiuses (radii) are the same size.

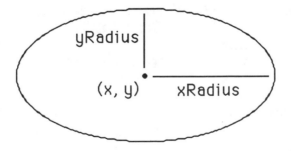

Here is a procedure to draw a circular ball that is filled with color.

```
procedure drawball (x, y, radius, Color: int)
    drawoval (x, y, radius, radius, Color)
    drawfill (x, y, Color, Color)
end drawball
```

To draw only a piece of a closed oval curve, what is called an **arc**, you use a instruction of the form:

```
drawarc (x, y, xRadius, yRadius, initialAngle, finalAngle,
        Color)
```

where the arc drawn is shown in the figure.

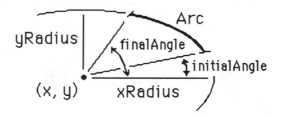

Here is a program to draw a piece of pizza. We will color it red. (It has a simple tomato sauce to start.) Our piece is to be one-sixth of a whole pizza. We can draw it as a series of red arcs. We will create a procedure called *drawslice*.

Here is the procedure:

```
procedure drawslice (x, y, radius, initialAngle,
                finalAngle, Color: int)
    for size: 1 .. radius
        drawarc (x, y, size, size,  initialAngle,
                finalAngle, Color)
    end for
end drawslice
```

Here are the instructions that use this procedure to draw the slice that starts at the mid-horizontal and goes down below the horizontal to the right of its center. We will draw the biggest pizza we can get on the screen. For this, the radius is *maxy* **div** 2

```
% The "pizza" program
% Draws a slice of pizza
(copy procedure drawslice here)
const radius := maxy div 2
const red := 4
drawslice (maxx div 2, maxy div 2, radius, 300, 0, red)
```

We could decorate our pizza with slices of mushroom caps or pepperoni. These could be little brown balls and we could use our *drawball* procedure placing them randomly on the slice.

Actually, Turing has a built-in procedure called *drawfillarc* that could be used to produce the same result as *drawslice*. (See Appendix 2.)

Random Positions

To calculate a random point on the screen say (*randx, randy*) we could use the predefined procedure *randint*. Here is a piece of a program that plots a dot at a random point on the screen.

```
var randx, randy: int
const red := 4
randint (randx, 0, maxx)
randint (randy, 0, maxy)
drawdot (randx, randy, red)
var reply : string (1)
getch (reply)
```

The first call to *randint* randomly assigns to *randx* an integer between *0* and *maxx* inclusive. Any one value in the range is equally likely (or equally probable).

Each time this program is run, the dot would be in exactly the same place on the screen. To get different random numbers from *randint* you must include the instruction *randomize* before the *randint* instruction is used. Try adding this to the program and running it several times. The dot will be in a different position each time you run the program. Here is a program that plots dots randomly on the screen in random colors.

```
% The "sprinkle" program
% Plots randomly colored dots randomly
% over the whole screen
var randx, randy, randcolor: int
const blue := 1
const yellow := 14
randomize
loop
    randint (randx, 0, maxx)
    randint (randy, 0, maxy)
    randint (randcolor, blue, yellow)
    drawdot (randx, randy, randcolor)
end loop
```

This program would have to be interrupted as it has an endless loop.

You could use the predefined constant *maxcolor* to set the random color using

```
randint (randcolor, 0, maxcolor)
```

Each time this program runs, the result would be a different sequence of random positions. When *randint* is used, each random number is produced in sequence from the previous random number. The beginning of the sequence is always the same unless we use *randomize*. This has the effect of producing a random starting number or **seed** for the sequence. The numbers are not really random but appear to be so. We say it is a sequence of **pseudo-random** numbers.

Errors that you might make

- Trying to use a nonexistent predefined procedure *drawcircle*.

- Not knowing how to express the angles in drawing an arc of an oval.

- Not putting in both the *xRadius* and *yRadius* in drawing a circle or the arc of a circle.

- Not being able to use *randint* properly. Forgetting to declare the variable to be given a random integer value.

- Forgetting to include the *randomize* statement if you want the random sequence of numbers to change from one run to the next.

Problems

1.   Write a program to draw a slice of pizza with brown pepperoni slices randomly distributed on it. Use about eight pieces of pepperoni on the slice. Use the built-in Turing procedure *drawfillarc*.

2.   Using the grid idea, write a program to place a random shape: ball, block, or triangle, in each square of the grid. The ball should just touch the sides. The triangle should use the lower boundary as base and touch the top. The block fills the grid square.

3.   Write a program to place randomly colored blocks in random grid squares in an endless loop.

4.   Write a program to draw a pattern in each square of the grid. The pattern is to be a red ball with a blue block fitted inside so its corners are just touching the outline of the ball. The ball itself just touches the grid block edges.

5.   Write a program to draw a small blue ball at the center of the screen and then by drawing successively larger blue circles have the ball grow in size until it touches the top and bottom of the screen.

6.   Write a program to draw a slice of watermelon with red flesh and green rind that is a quarter of a circular slice. Have it sitting on the bottom of the screen with its pointed part straight up in the air. Can you add seeds? (Use black circles.)

Animation

Any graphic can be erased by redrawing it in black which is the normal background color and has a color number of 0.

You can create the illusion that the graphic is moving by drawing it in one position, erasing it, and then drawing it in a new position. Usually we insert a delay between drawing and erasing so that it is slow enough to see.

Here is a program that has a ball start at the center of the screen and move diagonally up at a 45° angle until it hits the edge of the screen. It then bounces off the edge and is reflected like a hockey puck from the boards. It keeps on doing this.

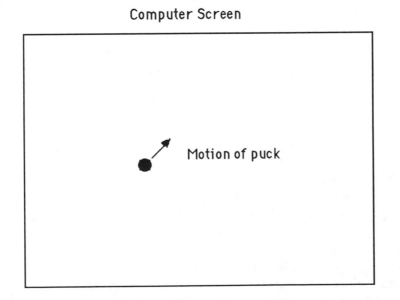

Computer Screen

We will use the predefined procedure *delay* to produce the delay between drawing and erasing. It has the form

```
delay (duration)
```

where the delay is in milliseconds (in multiples of 55 milliseconds which is the smallest detectable time). We will use delay (100) which produces a delay of about a tenth of a second.

```
% The "hockey" program gives the illusion of
% a red ball starting at the center
% of the screen and moving diagonally,
% bouncing off one edge of the screen
% and then another like a hockey puck.
% Start at center
var x := maxx div 2
var y := maxy div 2
% Set to move diagonally up
var xchange := 1
var ychange := 1
const red := 4
const black := 0
const size := 5

procedure drawball (x, y, size, Color: int)
    drawfilloval (x, y, size, size, Color)
end drawball

loop
    % When ball touches left or right edge
    if x = maxx or x = 0 then
        % Reflect horizontally
        xchange := -xchange
    end if
    % When ball touches the top or bottom edge
    if y = maxy or y = 0 then
        % Reflect vertically
        ychange := -ychange
    end if
```

```
        drawball (x, y, size, red)
        delay (100)
        drawball (x, y, size, black)
        % Move to a new position
        x := x + xchange
        y := y + ychange
    end loop
```

Changing Background Color

You can change the background color for pixel graphics using the instruction

```
        colorback (colorNumber)
```

The standard background color is black, so this is the color you use to erase a drawing. When the instruction *cls* is used with pixel graphics, the screen is cleared to the current background color. Here is a program that changes the screen color randomly every half second.

```
        % The "flash" program
        % Changes the screen color
        % randomly at half second intervals
        setscreen ("graphics")
        var randcolor: int
        randomize
        const black := 0
        const bright := 15
        loop
            randint (randcolor, black, bright)
            colorback (randcolor)
            cls
            delay (500)
        end loop
```

Since *cls* and *colorback* are both used with character graphics, the screen is not automatically switched to the pixel mode unless we use the instruction

setscreen ("graphics:cga")

for CGA graphics or

setscreen ("graphics:vga")

for VGA graphics.

The pixel graphics mode is automatically initiated by any of the instructions *drawdot*, *drawline*, *drawbox*, *drawoval*, and so on. It is only in this case that we need to use *setscreen*.

Errors that you might make

• Forgetting to insert a delay between drawing and erasing a picture in animation.

• Changing the position of the drawing from one stage to another in animation by too large or too small an amount. The speed of apparent motion depends both on the delay use and the size of the position change.

• Forgetting to use the *setscreen* statement when no specific pixel graphics instruction is used.

Problems

1.   Write an animation program to show a red ball moving horizontally across the screen from left to right and then having it bounce back as a blue square block. This action is to continue repeatedly for 20 times in each direction.

2.   Write a program to show a circular red ripple moving out from the center until it touches the edge of the screen at the top and bottom and then shrink back with smaller circles going to the center like running a movie backward.

3.   Write a program like "hockey" but which moves the puck randomly from one position to the next until it reaches an edge of the screen.

Hint: Use values for *xchange* and *ychange* which are chosen randomly between −1 and +1 pixels. The movement will be like a fly buzzing in the box. Use a brown fly on a blue background.

4.   Write a program like the fly buzzing program that does not erase the positions of the "fly" but leaves a trail. As soon as the "fly" hits a boundary start it at the center again but change the color (randomly). Design the program so that 5 flights from center to border are recorded on the screen before execution finishes.

Questions for Discussion

1.   What is the importance of having the two functions *maxx* and *mayy* built into the Turing language?

2.   How would you go about drawing a graphic that consisted of an isosceles triangle that is to be built of balls the way oranges might be stacked up in a store?

3.   What is involved in producing a graphic of a stack of objects – balls and tilted blocks – one on top of the other?

4.   Can you think of any basic patterns that might be great to have in a library of graphic procedures? How would you arrange their definitions so that they could be any size, any color or colors, and at any point on the screen?

Technical Terms you should now know

coordinates
origin of coordinates
pixel position
maxx
maxy
drawdot
drawline
closed figure
drawbox
drawfill
getch
grid
reserved word

drawoval
drawarc
random numbers
randint
randomize
pseudo-random numbers
maxcolor
animation
delay
background color
CGA graphics
VGA graphics
setscreen

Chapter 12

STRUCTURED DATA TYPES: ARRAY, RECORD AND FILE

*. . . a group of similar pieces of data
may be stored in the memory
as a structured data type.*

So far all our data consisted of individual pieces of information. These might be of various basic data types. For example, a person's year of birth may be an integer, their salary a real number, and their address a string of characters. Each of these pieces was stored in a memory location called a variable that was the right size to contain the corresponding data type. Reservations of memory space were arranged by having declarations of the variables in the program.

In this chapter we will see how a group of similar pieces of data may be stored in the memory as a structured data type. The structure will be given a name, just as a simple variable is given a name, in a declaration.

We will look at two possible data structures: the list and the table. These are both called **arrays**. The entries in a list or table may be single elements or **records**. A record is a way of grouping a number of single elements of different data types together as a unit. As well we see how data can be stored as a **file** in the secondary memory: the disk.

Questions and Answers about Structured Data Types

Q.   When would you want to use a structured data type rather than a simple data type?

A.   When I have a group of similar pieces of information like a group of 100 exam marks.

Q.   Why can't each exam mark in the group be stored in a separate variable?

A.   Because I would have to think up a name for each of the variables, rather than just a name for the group.

Q.   What could you think of as individual names if you had to?

A.   Well, I could call them *mark1*, *mark2*, *mark3*, *mark4*, and so on, up to *mark100*.

Q.   What would the 5th mark in the group be?

A.   It would be *mark5*.

Q.   How would you distinguish one mark from another if you called the whole group *mark*.

A.   I could have a serial number associated with each individual member of the group: 1 with the first and 100 with the last.

Q.   This serial number is exactly what is used. Its called the **index** of the individual piece of information in the group. We write the 5th piece as *mark (5)* with the index in parentheses. What would the 100th piece be?

A.   It would be *mark (100)*.

Q.   What would the nth piece be?

A.   It would be *mark (n)*.

Q.   That is a general expression for any piece in the group. We get the name of the particular piece by putting its index value in the general expression instead of *n*. What piece of the *mark* structure would be referenced for *n* = 7?

A.   It would be *mark (7)*.

Lists

We will be looking at two types of structured data types. These are **lists** and **tables**. A list is a number of pieces of information which are organized sequentially by having a common name and having an index that distinguishes one from another. Here is an example of a list of friends

Zeta
Bill
Marina
Yiu

. . .

To store this information in the computer we would declare a variable that we could call *friend* to be a structured data type. We use the type **array** to do this. It has been a tradition in computer science to use the word **array** rather than the word *list*. If we have 50 friends that we want to store we would use this declaration

var friend: **array** 1 .. 50 **of string**

The name of the variable that is to be a structured data type is followed by a colon, then the keyword **array**. After that is the range of the index values for the array, namely 1 to 50. Then follows the keyword **of** and the data type that each element of the array will have, which here is **string**. Remember they all must have the same data type.

Here is a picture of the array with names stored in it.

```
            ┌──────────────┐
            │ Zeta         │  friend(1)
            ├──────────────┤
            │ Bill         │  friend(2)
  The       ├──────────────┤
  friend    │ Marina       │  friend(3)
  array     ├──────────────┤
            │ Yiu          │  friend(4)
            ├──────────────┤
            │ ...          │
            │              │
            ├──────────────┤
            │ Maia         │  friend(50)
            └──────────────┘
```

We could store the information in the array by assignment statements of this sort.

```
friend (1) := "Zeta"
friend (2) := "Bill"
friend (3) := "Marina"
friend (4) := "Yiu"
  (and so on for all 50 friends.)
```

Another way is to read in the names from the keyboard. This can be done using a counted loop in this way:

```
% The "readlist" program
% Reads a list of 50 friends' names and
% stores them in an array data structure
var friend: array 1 .. 50 of string
put "Enter 50 names"
for count: 1 .. 50
    get friend (count)
end for
% Verify that you have read the list in
% by outputting it in sequence
for count: 1 .. 50
    put friend (count)
end for
```

We are able to take advantage of the power of the array structure. In the counted **for** loop the reference to the array element *friend (count)* will be different for each value of the counting index *count.* When *count* is 1 we read *friend (1)*; when count is 2 we read *friend (2)* and so on. We output the list in sequence to verify that it has been read in.

Initializing an Array in its Declaration

We have shown two ways of giving values to the elements of an array. A third way is to give values to the elements in the array's declaration. Here is an example where the array *month* is given values of the names of the months.

```
var month: array 1 .. 12 of string :=
    init ("Jan", "Feb", "Mar", "Apr", "May",
        "June", "July","Aug", "Sept", "Oct",
        "Nov", "Dec")
```

Or we could initialize an array of the names of the days of the week with this declaration:

```
var day: array 1 .. 7 of string := init  ("Mon",
    "Tues", "Wed", "Thu", "Fri", "Sat", "Sun")
```

Outputting a List Backwards

We can output a list just as easily as we read it in. And we could output it backwards if we wanted to. To do that we would add this to our previous program

```
for decreasing count: 50 .. 1
    put friend (count)
end for
```

Sorting a List

It is often useful to have a list sorted in some order. For example, a grocery list might be sorted in categories of food that are near each other in the supermarket in order to make shopping easy.

We often use lists to look up information. For instance, you might want to know if your list of friends contains a certain name. To find out, you would look either randomly or systematically. If you look systematically you would start at the beginning and look at one name after the other in the sequence. When you have found it you would stop looking.

It is a lot easier to find things if the list is in some kind of order, such as alphabetic order.

Here is an example with five names that are unsorted on the left but sorted into alphabetic order on the right.

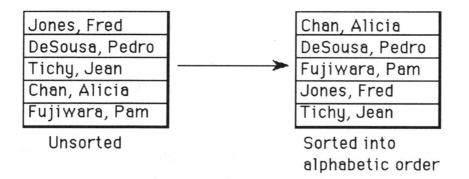

| Jones, Fred |
| DeSousa, Pedro |
| Tichy, Jean |
| Chan, Alicia |
| Fujiwara, Pam |

Unsorted

| Chan, Alicia |
| DeSousa, Pedro |
| Fujiwara, Pam |
| Jones, Fred |
| Tichy, Jean |

Sorted into
alphabetic order

To achieve this ordering we must sort the list. The problem is: how will we sort it? There are many different ways. It depends on whether or not we have lots of room in the computer's memory, and whether or not we care how long the sorting process takes. The computer can do it and, if we do not care about how efficiently it does it, we can use many different methods. The first method we will describe is **sorting by selection**.

Sorting by Selection

In sorting by selection, we will use a second array and place elements of our original array, one by one, into their sorted position in the second array.

To do this, we must be able to select the element of the original array that is to be moved next to the sorted array. We will always move the smallest (alphabetically least) element next. This means that if we had a subprogram for selecting the least element of an array we could use it. Here is such a subprogram. It can be written as a function *where* because we need only to know where the smallest element is located in the original array. If we know the location, we can move it to the sorted list and can eliminate it from being chosen again. To eliminate it, we would store a piece of data in the element that would never be chosen. We choose it to be "*zzz*" because that will never be chosen alphabetically least.

Here is an example with four names sorted by selection. First we select Alice, then Bob, then Cathy and finally Doug.

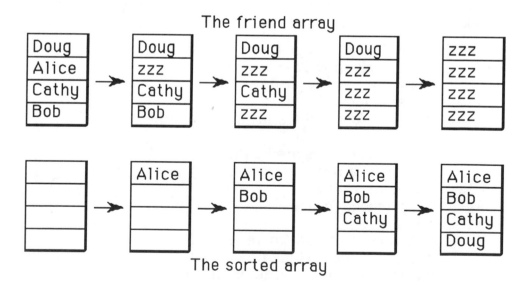

The friend array

The sorted array

Here is the procedure for finding the alphabetically least element:

```
% Finds alphabetically last element
function where (friend: array 1 .. * of string,
            size: int): int
    var least := friend (1)
    var place: int := 1
    for count: 2 .. size
        if friend (count) < least then
        least := friend (count)
        place := count
        end if
    end for
    result place
end where
```

When you have an array as a parameter of a subprogram you do not need to specify the upper end of the range of the index. You can just use an asterisk. We include the actual length of the array as a parameter *size.*

Here is the program that uses the function *where* to sort the array by selection.

```
% The "select" program
% Sorts an array by selection
(copy where function here)
var size: int
put "How long is the array to be sorted?"
get size
% Read in the unsorted array
var friend: array 1 .. size of string
for count: 1 .. size
    get friend (count)
end for
% Select smallest elements one at a time
% Placing them in the array sorted
var sorted: array 1 .. size of string
for count: 1 .. size
    var place := where (friend, size)
    % Move smallest element to sorted
```

```
            sorted (count) := friend (place)
            % Replace entry in original list by "zzz"
            friend (place) := "zzz"
        end for
        % Output sorted list
        for count: 1 .. size
            put sorted (count)
        end for
```

Input and Output with a Disk File

We have shown how to input an array that is a list from the keyboard, and output it to the screen. We can instead input it from a disk file and output it to a disk file.

We have seen how to input a program and save it on the disk. Lists of data can be input and saved on the disk in exactly the same way using the Turing editor. When data is stored on the disk, we often want to move it into the memory of the computer so that it can be changed in some way and then to write it back on the disk. This saves it for future use.

Suppose that we want to read in a list of names and sort them into alphabetic order, then record them back on the disk. We will start by entering the names using the Turing editor, then store them on the disk in a file named *people*. The full names will be entered with the last name first then a comma followed by a first name and any initials or other names. Each person's name will be on a separate line.

Here is the program that reads the names from the file *people*, into an array in the memory. Sorts the names alphabetically, and then outputs the sorted list. We will use three subprograms. The sorting will be by selection.

```
% The "readsort" program
% Reads names off a disk file
% named 'people' and stores them
% in an array named 'friend'.
% The list 'friend' is then sorted and written
% on a disk file named 'ordered'.
% There will be a maximum of 200 names
var friend : array 1 .. 200 of string (40)
var count: int

procedure readlist (var list: array 1 .. * of string (*),
              var count: int, filename: string)
    var filenumber: int
    open : filenumber, filename, get
    assert filenumber > 0
    count := 0
    loop
        exit when eof (filenumber)
        count := count + 1
        get: filenumber, list (count): *
    end loop
end readlist

function where (list: array 1 .. * of string (*),
                count: int): int
    var place: int := 1
    var least := list (1)
    for i: 2 .. count
        if list (i) < least then
            least := list (i)
            place := i
        end if
    end for
    result place
end where

procedure sort (var list: array 1 .. * of string (*),
                    count: int)
    var sorted: array 1 .. count of string (40)
    for i: 1 .. count
```

```
        var place := where (list, count)
        sorted (i) := list (place)
        list (place) := "zzz"
    end for
    % Move 'sorted' array back to 'list' array
    for i: 1 .. count
        list (i) := sorted (i)
    end for
end sort

procedure writelist (list: array 1 .. * of string (*),
                    count: int, filename: string)
    var filenumber: int
    open: filenumber, filename, put
    assert filenumber > 0
    for i: 1 .. count
        put: filenumber, list (i)
    end for
end writelist

readlist (friend, count, "people")
sort (friend, count)
writelist (friend, count, "ordered")
```

In this program we have used the **open** statement. The effect of using this is to assign a filenumber to a named disk file, for example the statement

open: filenumber, filename, **get**

will open the file given by the *filename* with a stream number *filenumber*. This *filenumber* must be declared as an integer variable. It is opened for reading because we have the keyword **get**. Then, when a **get** instruction to read from the file is given, it must have a colon after the **get**, then the *filenumber*, then a comma, and the list of what items are to be read.

If the process of opening a file fails, a zero will be assigned to the filenumber. That is why we have the statement

assert filenumber > 0

If the filenumber assigned is zero, the program will immediately stop.

To open a disk file for output, we use the keyword **put** in the **open** statement. Notice that in the parameters of the subprograms we could express the range of the array as 1 .. *. We can also use **string** (*) instead of **string** (40).

In the declaration of the local variable *sorted* in the *sort* procedure, we had to use definite values for the array range and the number of characters in the string.

Related Lists

Sometimes we have two lists that are related to each other. For example, you may have a list of friends and a list of their telephone numbers. When we have this situation, we use two arrays say *friend* and *phone*. The lists are arranged so that *friend* (1) has *phone* (1) as the number, *friend* (2) has *phone* (2), and so on.

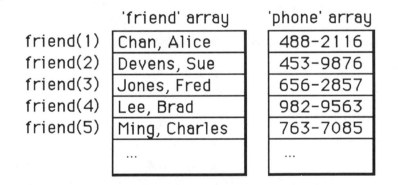

We will now look at the problem of storing such lists on the disk and using them to look up the phone number of a friend. Here our problem will be solved by having 2 subprograms: a procedure called *readlist* to read the lists from the disk; and a function called *spot* to look up the friend in the directory. We do not have to write the list back on the disk unless we change it.

We will write the program to accommodate a maximum of 200 friends. Here is the program:

```
% The "number" program
% Reads data on friends and phone numbers
% from a disk file 'book'
% and looks up any friend's number
var friend: array 1 .. 200 of string (40)
var phone: array 1 .. 200 of string (8)
var count: int

procedure readlists (
                var friend: array 1 .. * of string (40),
                var phone: array 1 .. * of string (8),
                var count: int, filename: string)
    var filenumber: int
    open: filenumber, filename, get
    assert filenumber > 0
    count := 0
    loop
        exit when eof (filenumber)
        count := count + 1
        get: filenumber, friend (count): 40,
                  phone (count): 8, skip
    end loop
end readlists
```

```
function spot (name: string,
               friend: array 1 .. * of string (40),
               count: int): int
    var place : int := 0
    var nameWithSpaces : string
    % Make name have 40 characters
    nameWithSpaces := name +
            repeat (" ", 40 – length (name))
    for i: 1 .. count
        if nameWithSpaces = friend (i) then
            place := i
            exit
        end if
    end for
    result place
end spot

% This is the rest of the main program
readlists (friend, phone, count, "book")
var name: string
loop
    put "Enter name to be looked up, 'zzz' to stop"
    get name: *
    exit when name = "zzz"
    const place := spot (name, friend, count)
    put "phone number of ", name, " is " ..
    if place not= 0 then
        put phone (place)
    else
        put "unlisted"
    end if
end loop
```

In the *spot* function we must pad the name on the right with blanks so that it is 40 characters long. To be equal to each other, two strings must be of exactly the same length.

Frequency Distributions

In preparing a summary of information we sometimes create charts of the statistics. These charts are often **frequency distributions**. For example, if the basic information is a set of exam marks out of 100, we might prepare a chart showing how frequently each mark was obtained. There might be 5 times that the mark 65 was obtained, 3 times that the mark 82 was obtained, and so on. Usually we chart the frequency of a range of marks like the 50s, the 60s, the 70s, and so on. In each range there will be a number of occurrences. In this way we get an idea of how the marks are distributed; we get meaningful statistical information.

Here is a program that generates 100 simulated test marks out of a total of 10, and, from these, prepares a frequency distribution for each possible mark. The results are then displayed as a chart of asterisks, each asterisk representing a single occurrence of a mark. There will be 100 asterisks distributed among the 11 different possible test results.

```
% The "statistics" program
% Prepares a frequency distribution
% of simulated test marks
% and displays it as a chart
var freq: array 0 .. 10 of int :=
              init (0,0,0,0,0,0,0,0,0,0,0)
randomize
var test: int
for count: 1 .. 100
    randint (test, 0, 10)
    freq (test) := freq (test) + 1
end for
% Output chart of asterisks
put "Frequency distribution of test marks"
for value: 0 .. 10
    put value, " ", repeat ("*", freq (value))
end for
```

Here is a sample execution:

```
 0 *********
 1 **********
 2 *********
 3 ********
 4 *********
 5 ********
 6 *********
 7 ********
 9 **********
10 *********
```

The distribution is nearly uniform, that is, there are approximately the same number of asterisks for each test value. This is no surprise because the *randint* procedure is supposed to produce a uniform distribution. But in any such distribution there are **fluctuations**; some values have fewer asterisks than others, some more. These fluctuations become relatively less noticeable as you get a larger number of values. If you had 200 values, instead of 100, the fluctuations as a percentage of the total would be smaller. This is a characteristic of statistical results.

Problems

1.   Prepare a disk file of 100 random integers between 0 and 100 storing it as a file named *exam*.

2.   Use the file *exam* prepared in question 1 to find the median mark. Remember: half of the marks are above the median and half below.

3.   Write a program to read a file of integers, such as *exam,* sort them in ascending order, and store them back on the disk as *sortexam.* Use a file of 500 randomly generated integers between 0 and 100 to start.

4.   Prepare two files of 100 sorted integers. Sort them into a single file of 200 integers by **merging** the two files of 100.

5.   A catalog for a clothing store contains two related lists of: items for sale and their price. Prepare a small catalog on a disk file called *catalog*. Write a program to prepare a bill for a purchase of items from the catalog entered by the user at the keyboard. The total bill is to include 15% sales tax on the total.

6.   Write a program to simulate the throwing of two dice over and over and keeping a frequency distribution of the results. Output the distribution for 100 throws of the two dice. Is the distribution a uniform one?

7.   Write a program that takes, as input, any date in this century in the form

        3   17   23

and outputs it in this form

        March 17, 1923

Tables

A table is a display of information entries in rows and columns. Each entry in the table must be of the same data type.

As an example of a table we will think of one to store exam marks: each row of marks is for a different student; each column represents a different course. There will be 100 students and 5 courses for each.

Five courses

	1	2	3	4	5
1	78	76	89	64	82
2	82	87	89	79	90
3	67	70	76	68	64
4	91	89	94	88	94
5	67	70	68	59	73
6	88	80	77	79	75
7	87	83	89	73	89
...					

100 students

The 'mark' array

We are assuming every student takes the same set of 5 courses. If we call the table *mark* it would be declared in this way:

var *mark*: **array**: 1 .. 100, 1 .. 5 **of int**

The mark for the 50th student in the list in course number 4 would be found by *mark* (50, 4).

We can read in a table of marks of this type by this program:

```
% The "inmark" program
% Reads in a table of marks
% a row at a time
var mark: array 1 .. 100, 1 .. 5 of int
put "Enter marks, for each student for 100 students"
for student: 1 .. 100
    for course: 1 .. 4
        get mark (student, course)
    end for
end for
```

We could read in the marks a column at a time by reversing the two **for** statements. To be useful, such a table of marks would have to have a related list of names of the students.

Problems

1.   Prepare a table of exam marks called *mark* for students by generating them randomly. Use only 10 students and 5 courses. Add an extra column to the table we had to hold the student's average mark in the 5 courses and an extra row to hold the class' average in each course. The table will thus have after you finish the calculation, 6 columns and 11 rows. What will the entry for

mark (11, 6)

contain?

2.   How could you sort the table so that the students were ranked on the basis of their average marks?

Records

Very often we are required to sort related arrays such as the ones giving our friends' names and phone numbers. All methods of sorting require you to move the individual units that are being sorted from one location to another in the memory. This means that you must move both the phone number and the name.

In Turing there is a way of grouping elements together so they can be moved about in the memory as a unit. This is the **record** structure. In the telephone list instead of two related lists, we would have a single list of records, each record containing the name and phone number that are related.

Suppose we had a single record called *entry* which contained a name and phone number.

It would be declared this way:

> **var** entry:
>   **record**
>   friend: **string** (40)
>   phone: **string** (8)
>   **end record**

We say the record *entry* has two fields. We refer to the individual fields by joining the name of the record and the name of the field with a period. For example

> entry.friend := "Bill"

would assign the name *Bill* to that field of the record.

> entry.phone := "880–1167"

would assign the number 880-1167 to that field of the record.

```
friend       phone
┌────────┬──────────────┐
│  Bill  │   880-1167   │
└────────┴──────────────┘
```
The 'entry' record

We can move both fields from where they are to another memory location provided that it has the same data type. Here is an example:

> **var** temp:
>   **record**
>   friend: **string** (40)
>   phone: **string** (8)
>   **end record**

This means *temp* has the same data type as *entry*. To save writing this twice, we can define a data type once and then say that both *entry* and *temp* have this data type.

Here it is with a **type definition** included:

type entryType:
    record
        friend: **string** (40)
        phone: **string** (8)
    end record
    var entry: entryType
    var temp: entryType

We can have a list of 20 such records with this declaration

    var phonebook: **array** 1 .. 20 **of** entryType

We can illustrate the phonebook array this way.

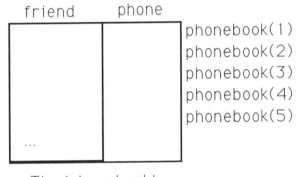

The 'phonebook'
array of records

To exchange (or swap) two records in this phone book, for instance, the 5th and the 82nd, we can use these instructions:

    temp := phonebook (82)
    phonebook (82) := phonebook (5)
    phonebook (5) := temp

The record is moved as a unit.

Unfortunately records cannot be read in or output as a unit, but must be handled a field at a time. To output the 20th record of the phone book to the screen we would write

    put phonebook(20).friend: 40, phonebook (20).phone: 8

Errors that you might make

- Not including the correct number of values for the elements of the array when using **init**.

- Not using the * properly in giving the index range of an array in a subprogram's parameter list.

- Forgetting the colon after the keyword **open**.

- Forgetting to declare the *filenumber* as an integer variable.

- Forgetting the *:filenumber* in an input or output instruction where a disk file is involved.

- Forgetting to have the filenumber in parentheses after an *eof*.

- Trying to test the equality of two strings of different lengths.

- Expecting frequency distributions to give exactly equal frequencies for values generated from uniform distributions.

- Mixing up rows and columns of a table.

- Forgetting **end record** in the definition of a record type.

- Confusing a type definition with a variable declaration.

- Trying to input or output records as a unit rather than field by field.

- Putting the array index in the wrong place in referring to a field in an array of records: writing **put** phonebook.friend (20).

Problems

1.   Adapt the program *readsort* of this chapter to work for the phone book. You will be sorting it alphabetically by your friends' names.

2.   What changes would you make to have the phone book sorted by telephone numbers instead of by friends' names?

Questions for Discussion

1.   A good rule to go by in programming is to choose as simple a data structure as possible. For example, you should not use an array if you could get along with just simple variables. Why is this a good principle?

2.   What advantage is there in using an array of records over using several related simple arrays?

3.   How might you write a program to draw a bar chart, using pixel graphics, from a frequency distribution that you might calculate?

4.   In what ways would drawing a pie chart from a frequency distribution be harder than drawing a bar chart?

5.   If the assertion made in an **assert** statement is not true at the time it is reached in program execution, the execution stops. Why is stopping execution not a good thing in a piece of commercial software?

Technical Terms you should now know

array

list

table

index of array

look up

open

assert

filenumber

filename

related lists

row

column

record

record data type

field of record

type definition

type

Chapter 13

SOLVE AN EASY PROBLEM FIRST

*The technique is to simplify
the problem that you want to solve
so that it becomes easy to solve.*

Now that you have been introduced to the use of lists and tables of the array data type, and to files of data on disk, we can attempt some more difficult problems.

This permits us to look at a new problem-solving technique.

The technique is to simplify the problem that you want to solve so that it becomes easy to solve.

Then, by making changes to the solution of the easier problem, we can create a solution to the original harder problem.

We can then add this to our repertoire of problem-solving techniques: analogy, systematic, divide and conquer, and so on.

Questions and Answers about Simplification

Q.   You are given a problem of forming two more or less equal baseball teams from a list of players each of whom has a detailed record of performance in past games. How could you simplify this problem?

A.   I could ignore the past performances and just divide the list randomly into two parts.

Q.   Would the two teams be as equal as you could make them?

A.   I could do this several times and see after I did it whether the teams were equal and choose the one where they are matched most closely.

Q.   How are you going to judge whether two players are equal?

A.   I could add up their performance figures and get an average for each player.

Q.   Knowing the average performance figure for each player could you devise a new method of dividing them so that you get more or less equal teams?

A.   I could arrange (sort) the list of available players in order of descending performance merit. Then I would put the first on the list on team 1, the second on team 2, the third on team 1, the fourth on team 2, and so on.

Q.   This should give teams with approximately the same average performance figure. But obviously the first team will be better because every one of its players has a higher performance record than the player chosen next by team 2. What might you try to do to see that this did not happen?

A.   I could decide at random before each pair of choices which team is to choose first.

Q.   I think you are beginning to see how you start by solving an easy problem and gradually change the solution so that you are solving a harder problem.

An Example of Solving an Easy Problem First

Here is the problem: The text of an essay is stored in a disk file. Devise a program to read the text and format it so that it is left and right justified on the page. The maximum width of the line is to be specified by the user.

We will begin by simplifying the problem so that it places the text in lines that are left justified with no more characters than the maximum width but which are not also right justified. Here is a program that will do this:

```
% The "format1" program
% Asks the user to enter the name
% of a disk file to be formatted
% It asks also for the maximum line width
var filein, fileout : string
var filenumberin, filenumberout : int
var maxLength : int
put "What file do you want to format?"
get filein
open : filenumberin, filein, get
% If "open" fails it sets the filenumber to 0
assert filenumberin > 0
put "In what file is the formatted file to be stored?"
get fileout
open : filenumberout, fileout, put
assert filenumberout > 0
put "What is the maximum line width?"
get maxLength
var word, line : string
if not eof (filenumberin) then
    get : filenumberin, line
end if
loop
    exit when eof (filenumberin)
    get : filenumberin, word
    if length (word) + length (line) >= maxLength then
        put : filenumberout, line
        line := word
```

```
        else
            line := line + " " + word
        end if
    end loop

    % Output last line
    put : filenumberout, line
```

Solving the Harder Problem

Now we must face up to the more difficult problem of both left and right justifying the line. To do this we must store the words that will make up the line in an array and then, when another word would cause the line to overflow the maximum with just one blank after each word, we must output the line. Before we do we must add some blanks after words in the array so that the last word will be at the right margin of the line.

Here are the changes starting just after the *maxLength* has been read.

```
    var word: array 1 .. 30 of string
    var count, lengthLine: int := 0
    var wordin: string
    ( include procedure "outputLine" here)

    % Place randomly
    randomize

    loop
        exit when eof (filenumberin)
        get : filenumberin, wordin
        if length (wordin) + lengthLine > maxLength then
            var blanks := maxLength - lengthLine + count
            outputLine (count, word, blanks, filenumberout)
            word (1) := wordin
            count := 1
            lengthLine := length (wordin) + 1
        else
            count := count + 1
```

```
            word (count) := wordin
            lengthLine := lengthLine + length (wordin) + 1
        end if
    end loop

% Output last line
for i : 1 .. count
    put : filenumberout, word (i)
end for

loop
    exit when eof (filenumberin)
    get: filenumberin, wordin
    if length (wordin) + lengthLine > maxLength then
        var blanks := maxLength – lengthLine
        outputLine (count, word, blanks, filenumberout)
        word (1) := wordin + " "
        count := 1
        lengthLine := length (wordin) + 1
    else
        count := count + 1
        word (count) := wordin + " "
        lengthLine := lengthLine + length (wordin) + 1
    end if
end loop

% Output last line
for i: 1 .. count
    put: filenumberout, word (i) + " "
end for
```

We have not yet written the subprogram *outputLine*. In it we must distribute the blanks among the array of words and then output the words with the distributed blanks. The problem is: how do you distribute the blanks. If there are more blanks than words you would put at least one blank on every word and then distribute the rest.

Placing the blanks in position is a difficult problem. Suppose you chose to place them at the end of each word starting with the first word until there are no more? In this case, the output would have more blanks between words at the beginning of the line in every line. This looks bad. If you look at the pages in this book perhaps you can see where the blanks have been placed. We will take the easy way out by placing the blanks randomly among the words. Here is the subprogram:

```
procedure outputLine (count : int,
                var word : array 1 .. * of string,
                var blanks : int, filenumberout : int)
    % Number of words is given by count
    % Number of places for blanks is count -1
    const places := count - 1
    if places > 0 then
        if blanks > places then
            % Add a blank to every place
            for i : 1 .. places
                word (i) := word (i) +
                        repeat (" ", blanks div places)
            end for
            % Compute blanks remaining to be placed
            blanks := blanks mod places
        end if
        var spot : int
        for i : 1 .. blanks
            randint (spot, 1, places)
            word (spot) := word (spot) + " "
        end for
    end if
    % Output the line
    for i: 1 .. count
        put: filenumberout, word (i) ..
    end for
    % Finish line
    put: filenumberout, ""
end outputLine
```

Another Example of Solving an Easy Problem First

You are told that the computer time required to sort a list of N items by most methods is greater than the total time taken to sort the two halves of the list (each consisting of N/2 items) separately and then merging the two halves into a single sorted list.

Here is a problem where we will put off thinking about how we will sort the two halves and will just merge two lists. This is an easier problem. The two lists will be stored in the same array called *list* starting at the index *first* and ending at the index *last*. The first sorted list goes from index *first* to index *middle*. The second list goes from *middle* to *last*.

Here is an example of a list that contains 8 elements. The middle element is number 4. Elements 1 to 4 are in order and so are elements 5 to 8. We start by comparing element 1 to element 5 and we copy the smallest of these, which is 12, to the temp array. Next we compare element 2 to element 5, and copy the smallest. This continues until all elements have been copied, in order of size, to the temp array.

list

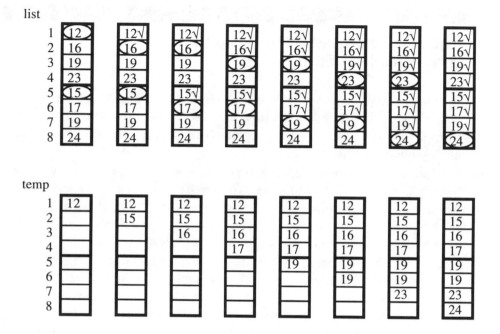

temp

The merged list will be placed back in the same place in the array and will be sorted from *first* to *last*. We will write the merging as a procedure called *merge* and use an array of integers:

```
procedure merge (var list: array 1 .. * of int,
                 first, middle, last: int)
    % Merges two sorted arrays of integers
    % one going from first to middle the other
    % from middle + 1 to last
    % Declare a temporary array to
    % store merged arrays
    var temp: array 0 .. last - first of int
    % Initialize pointers to two sorted lists
    var point1 := first
    var point2 := middle + 1
    for point3: first .. last
        % point3 locates item in merged list
        if point1 < middle + 1 and (point2 > last
```

```
            or list (point2) > list (point1)) then
                % Move item from first half
                temp (point3 – first) := list (point1)
                % Advance pointer 1
                point1 := point1 + 1
            else
                % Move item from second half
                temp (point3 – first) := list (point2)
                % Advance pointer 2
                point2 := point2 + 1
            end if
        end for
        % Copy merged array back to original place
        for point3: first .. last
            list (point3) := temp (point3 – first)
        end for
    end merge
```

We can now write a sketch of a subprogram that uses the *merge* procedure to sort. The subprogram is very short and is different from others we have looked at because it is going to call itself. You may find it difficult to follow but it actually works. Here it is:

```
    procedure mergeSort (var list: array 1 .. * of int,
                          first, last: int)
        if last > first then
            % Find middle
            const middle := (first + last) div 2
            Sort half from first to middle
            Sort half from middle + 1 to last
            merge (list, first, middle, last)
        end if
    end mergeSort
```

This program is able to operate provided that the list is at least two items long.

We can solve the hard problem of sorting the two halves of the list by using the *mergesort* procedure itself. This is what we call then a **recursive** subprogram. It uses itself.

We sort the first half by this call:

mergesort (list, first, middle)

and the second half with this instruction:

mergesort (list, middle + 1, last)

This looks really peculiar. We ask the computer to sort each half by a method that will ask it to divide that half in two and sort each half, naturally by the same method. It is a little like divide and conquer. We keep dividing the halves into half again and again until there is only one item left in each half and we then merge the two by the *merge* procedure. We call this a **recursive merge sort**. It is very efficient.

This is an example where we keep trying to solve an easier problem over and over again until it is no problem at all. We postpone facing up to the hard problem until there is no hard problem left. It has disappeared.

Sometimes solving an easy problem first is a very good way to attack a difficult problem.

Problems

In each of these problems try to find an easy problem to solve first.

1.   Write a program that will draw a series of 10 square boxes, one inside the next. The successive boxes are to be oriented so that their diagonals are at right angles to each other. Start with as large a box as you can draw.

2.   Write a program that draws as large a circle as possible, then a square box inside it, a circle inside that, then another square inside that. Arrange to draw as many as you can before it gets hopelessly small. All the boxes will have corresponding sides parallel to each other.

3.   Write a program to form two baseball teams by the various random methods suggested in the questions and answers of this chapter and compare the results.

Questions for Discussion

1.   What methods of sorting have been mentioned so far in this book? Can you think of any other possible methods?

2.   In text processors there are often spelling checkers. How might you go about writing a spelling checker program?

3.   In keeping files of records up to date, transactions that change records are often sorted in the same way as the records are sorted. How then might the updating of the file be accomplished?

4.   Does it always help to solve a simpler problem first? Can you think of examples?

Technical Terms you should now know

merge   recursive merge sort
recursive subprogram

Chapter 14

MUSIC

The kind of music that you can program in Turing ... is either a single note or a series of notes.

The music can be played without anything on the screen or it can accompany a graphic display

The kind of music that you can program in Turing is very simple. It is either a single note or a series of notes.

You cannot sound notes simultaneously to produce harmony.

Nevertheless, even simple melodies can enhance computer graphics or signal the progress of execution of a program.

Questions and Answers about Programming Music

Q.   What notation would you use to program a melody?

A.   I would give a series of notes, perhaps by using their letters A, B, C up to G.

Q.   Good suggestion. What else would you have to give?

A.   The time that each note is sounded; for say a whole note, or half note, or quarter note.

Q.   That is its duration. If you were using a sequence of characters to represent the notes where would the durations be?

A.   In a separate sequence with one duration corresponding to each note.

Q.   That is not the way we actually do it. We give the durations as numbers. Each note can be preceded by a single character giving its duration. How would we represent durations, such as a quarter note, by a single character?

A.   I could give the denominator of the fraction 4 for 1/4 note, 8 for 1/8 note, and so on.

Q.   That would be great. What about sharps and flats of the notes?

A.   I could add another character after the letter to indicate this .

Q.   We add a + for a sharp and a – for a flat because we do not have the characters # and b that are usually used.

Playing Musical Notes

Musical notes can be played one-at-a-time or as a series of notes. To play a single note we use the predefined procedure *play* in the form

> play (value-of-note)

where the value of note is its duration followed by its pitch. The pitch of a note is given by the letters A to G inclusive which represent the corresponding musical notes. (Little letters a to g can be used equally well.)

If the letter is followed by a plus sign, the note is sharp; if by a minus sign, the note is flat. For example, we can play the note D and then an F sharp this way:

> play ("D")
> play ("F+")

These notes are played as quarter notes. The duration of a note is given by a single digit according to this table:

> 1   whole note
> 2   half note
> 4   quarter note
> 8   eighth note
> 6   sixteenth note

So this plays C as an eighth note:

> play ("8C")

All subsequent notes will be eighth notes unless explicitly set to a different duration. The pitch is presumed to be in the middle octave which starts at middle C. The middle octave notes are

> C D E F G A B

To represent C in the octave above the middle octave, we use the notation >C. To represent it in the octave below the middle, we use <C. Once either > or < have been used all future notes in that *play* instruction, or in subsequent *play* instructions, are shifted to the same octave. To prevent the notation for one note from influencing the value of the next, we should make a practice of returning to the middle octave after the note is played.

For example, to play an eighth note with pitch A in the octave above the middle octave we would use

```
play ("8 > A<")
```

In these examples, the value of a note has been a string of characters which are enclosed in quotes. We could also write

```
var note := "8 >A<"
play (note)
```

Now the parameter of the *play* procedure is a string variable. Here is a program which plays random sixteenth notes in the C-scale in the middle octave

```
% The "longsong" program
% Plays sixteenth notes in C scale at random
const CScale := "CDEFGAB"
play ("6")  % Set to play sixteenth notes
var note: int
loop
    randint (note, 1, 7)  % Pick a note at random
    play (CScale (note))
end loop
```

Since all notes are to be with the same duration we can give a *play* statement to set this for all following notes. Notice that the parameter of *play* giving the value of the note is a one-character substring of the string *CScale*.

Resting for a While

Sometimes we want an interval of silence in our music. This is called a **rest** or **pause** and is achieved by playing a "note" whose "pitch" is P (or p). The duration of the rest is given in the same way as the duration of a note. A half note rest is given as "2p".

Playing a Series of Notes

A series of notes is given by catenating the notations for individual notes and placing the resulting string in a *play* instruction. If the duration is the same from one note to the next, it need not be repeated. If the octave is the same you do not need to return to the middle and then go back to the same octave. For example, the instruction

> play (">8A< >8B<")

which plays two notes, both eighth notes in the octave above the middle octave could be written more simply as

> play (">8AB<")

Notice that we make a practice of returning to the middle octave even after a series of notes. Here are two instructions that play "Mary had a little lamb"

> play ("4EDCDEE2E4DD2D4EG2G")
> play ("4EDCDEEEEDDED2C")

Using the Keyboard to Make Music

Here is a program that lets you play music using the keyboard of the computer. It plays the notes of the C-scale when you press the keys 1–8. When you press 1 you get middle C, when you press 2 you get D, and so on. When you press 8 you get C in the octave above the middle octave. All the notes have the same duration. Before you begin you will be asked to enter the digit that corresponds to the duration you want.

```
% The "piano" program
% Makes the keyboard into a musical keyboard
var duration: string (1)
put "Enter one digit to control duration"
put "You can enter 1, 2, 4, 8, or 6: " ..
get duration
play (duration)
put "You can now begin to play"
put "Play notes by pressing keys 1 to 8, ",
    "any other key to stop"
var note: string (1)
loop
    getch (note) % Wait until a key is pressed
    if note = "1" then
        play ("C")
    elsif note = "2" then
        play ("D")
    elsif note = "3" then
        play ("E")
    elsif note = "4" then
        play ("F")
    elsif note = "5" then
        play ("G")
    elsif note = "6" then
        play ("A")
    elsif note = "7" then
        play ("B")
    elsif note =  "8" then
```

```
            play (">C<")
      else
            exit
      end if
end loop
```

Try playing a simple folk tune on your keyboard. Record the notes so you can use them to write a program to play the tune automatically.

Animation with Music

In this section we will try a more difficult problem. We will combine animated graphics with music. It is important that the music and the graphics be in time with each other; they must be synchronized.

The particular problem we will attempt is a sing-along animation which displays the words of a song, one-line-at-a-time, and has a ball bounce from one syllable of the words to the next, as the corresponding note to be sung is played. This used to be a very common way of leading a sing song for a group of people sitting in a theatre.

- The problem will be simplified by treating all syllables as strings of length 7 characters (including any hyphen). This means that the "bouncing ball" can be placed above the first character of the string. If the line consists of 5 syllables with 5 corresponding notes, then the ball will be in column 1 for the first note, 8 for the next, 15 for the next, and so on, for 5 different positions.

- We will not try to animate the ball's motion between these positions in our simple program. It will just disappear from one position and reappear at the next when the note is finished playing. Here there is no need to have a delay in the animation; that is accomplished by waiting for *playdone* to be **true**. The predefined function *playdone* is a boolean function whose value is true if the last note of the preceding *play* procedure is finished.

- We will store the songs in a library of old favorites on the disk. These data files will have this form

> number of lines
> {number-of-syllables-in-line
>   syllables-separated-by-blanks
>   notes-separated-by-blanks }

- The individual line specifications are preceded by an integer which tells how many lines there are. Each line is preceded by the number of syllables in the line followed by those syllables, separated by blanks, then the corresponding notes, separated by blanks.

- Here is what the data would look like for the first verse of the song "Mary had a Little Lamb"

```
5
7   Ma- ry had a lit- tle lamb
    4E   4D 4C 4D  4E   4E  2E
3   Lit- tle lamb 4D 4D 2D
3   Lit- tle lamb 4E 4G 2G
7   Ma- ry had a lit- tle lamb
    4E   4D  4C  4D  4E   4E   4E
6   Its fleece was white as snow
    4E   4D  4D   4E   4D  2C
```

- The description of the notes is given so that each note is specified independently of the previous notes or the following notes. This means that each will have a duration and a pitch. If the note is not in the middle octave, then the pitch is preceded by the sign (or signs) necessary to shift octaves and followed by the complementary sign (or signs) to return to the middle octave.

- The maximum length of the string needed to specify a note is seven characters, one for duration, one or two for pitch, two or four for octave shift and return.

- If there is a pause, a syllable with no characters (null string) is inserted in the line. To do this you must use two double quotes with no characters between. The corresponding note will be a p (pause) prefaced by a duration.

- Since the line of the song must fit onto the line on the screen we will allow for a maximum of 11 syllables which would take up 77 character positions. Longer lines can be split into two. The syllables of the lines will be stored in a two-dimensional array called *lineSyll* where each element is

lineSyll (line, syllNo)

The 3rd syllable of the 2nd line would be

lineSyll (2, 3)

- We will read in the whole song from the disk before playing it so that any delays in getting it from the disk will not interrupt the playing of the song. Because the input is from the disk there are no prompts.

Here is a sketch of the program

```
% The "singsong" program
% Plays songs for a sing-a-long
% Read song from disk
for line: 1 .. numberOfLines
    % Display words of line on screen row 10
    for syll: 1 .. numberOfSyll (line)
        % Plot ball over syllable
        % Play corresponding note
        % When playdone = true erase ball
    end for
    % Erase words of line
end for
```

The number of syllables in the lines will be stored in a one-dimensional array called *numberOfSyll* where the element *numberOfSyll* (3) would be the number of syllables in the third line. Here is the complete program

```
% The "singsong" program
% Plays songs for a sing-a-long
% Read song from disk
var numberOfLines: int
get numberOfLines
var lineSyll: array 1 .. numberOfLines,
        1 .. 7 of string (7)
var lineNote: array 1 .. numberOfLines,
        1 .. 7 of string (7)
var numberOfSyll: array 1 .. numberOfLines of int
for line: 1 .. numberOfLines
    % Read number of syllables in line
    get numberOfSyll (line)
    % Read syllables in line
    for syllNo: 1 .. numberOfSyll (line)
        get lineSyll (line, syllNo)
    end for
    % Read notes in line
    for noteNo: 1 .. numberOfSyll (line)
        get lineNote (line, noteNo)
    end for
end for
cls
setscreen ("nocursor") % Hide cursor
for line: 1 .. numberOfLines
    % Display words of line on screen row 10
    locate (10, 1)
    for syllNo: 1 .. numberOfSyll (line)
        put lineSyll (line, syllNo): 7 ..
    end for
    % Plot ball over syllable
    for syllNo: 1 .. numberOfSyll (line)
        % Display ball over syllable in screen row
        locate (9, 1 + (syllNo − 1) * 7)
        put "*" ..
```

```
% Play corresponding note
play (lineNote (line, syllNo))
% When playdone is true, erase ball
loop
    exit when playdone
end loop
locate (9, 1 + (syllNo – 1) * 7)
put  " " ..
end for
% Erase words of line
locate (10, 1)
put " "
end for
```

If the song is stored in the file called *Mary* the program could be executed using the run command that redirects the input to be from that file.

The combination of music and graphics can be used to enhance many computer applications.

Problems

1.   Write a program to read in a string of symbols that represent a song you know, and then play it repeatedly.

2.   Arrange that there is a pause of 10 full notes duration between repetitions of the song of question 1.

3.   Arrange that you can interrupt the repetitions of the song of question 1 by typing the letter *q* for quit.

4.   Write a program to play a song and display the words a line-at-a-time (for a song of at least four lines). Do not display the words of the next line until the notes of the previous line have finished playing.

5.   Prepare the data (notes and words) for a song to be in the sing-a-long library for the program *singsong*. Store it on the disk. Now run the *singsong* program using your song as input data.

6.   Try to see if you can use a **case** statement, instead of a cascaded **if**...**then**...**elsif**...**else**statement in the *piano* program. Is it possible?

7.   Write a program like the *piano* program that lets you sound any of the 12 notes on the piano (including the black keys) in the middle octave at any duration that you want. This is not to be a program for playing at a normal rate but rather one that will provide you with a note to start a group singing without accompaniment.

8.   Write a program that sounds notes in the scale of three flats at random. This scale is E-flat major. The E-flat scale can be played with the instruction

   play ("E–FGA–B–>CDE–<")

9.   Write a program that plays Beethoven's "Ode to Joy" and at the same time changes the color of the screen every third note. Here is a string that represents the ode:

   8bb>cddc<baggabb6p
   a4a8bb>cddc<baggaba6p
   g4g8aabga6b>c<8bga6b>c
   <8baga4d
   8bb>cddc<baggaba6p
   g4g

Store the song on the disk in the one-note-at-a-time form. Read it into an array before you play it.

10.   Modify the program of question 9 to change screen color randomly so that the number of notes (or pauses) between color changes varies between 2 and 6.

11.   Improve the *singSong* program by inserting another position of the bouncing ball between syllables. Put this on row 8, half way between syllable positions.

Questions for Discussion

1.   The music making capabilities of Turing are quite limited. Is it worthwhile to have them at all?

2.   Computers are used in many ways for the composition and performance of music. Do you know about any of these?

3.   Simple tunes played on the computer can add humor to computer graphics. Can you think of any possible examples?

4.   If you are slow at playing on the computer "piano" for the program in this chapter how could the program be modified to record the notes you enter and then play them back at proper speed?

Technical Terms you should now know

octave   rest
pitch   pause
duration   flat
scale   sharp
play   *playdone*

Chapter 15

THE STEP-BY-STEP REFINEMENT
METHOD OF PROBLEM SOLVING

*. . . the problem of designing and
creating computer programs
has had a lot of attention.*

In this book we have been examining a number of different methods of problem solving and illustrating these methods by creating computer programs to solve problems.

At no time did we create a program to solve all problems. As far as we know no such program can be created. Different problems require different solutions.

We can identify types of problems and the problem of designing and creating computer programs is a type of problem that has had a lot of attention.

A method of designing programs that is extremely useful is the method of **step-by-step refinement** (sometimes called stepwise refinement). This method makes use of other methods we have introduced: both the systematic method, and the divide and conquer method.

Questions and Answers about Step-by-Step Refinement

Q.   When you think about solving a problem, what language are you using?

A.   I use English. (Some people use other natural languages.)

Q.   When you create a computer program, what language is it written in?

A.   I use Turing. (Some people use other programming languages.)

Q.   What is the thing you start with when you solve a problem?

A.   A statement of the problem specification.

Q.   Is this statement all in English?

A.   It could have some mathematical expressions as well, or parts that I could express mathematically.

Q.   To solve the problem you must translate the problem specification in English (and Mathematics) into a computer program in Turing. Could a computer do this for you?

A.   I do not think it could, because then it could solve any problem you could specify.

Q.   The computer can translate your Turing program into a language it understands, but that is because Turing is clearly defined. Are the steps from problem specification to Turing program clearly defined?

A.   No. I must think creatively to produce them.

The Step-by-Step Method

Helping you think creatively is what the step-by-step refinement method allows. You do not have to think of every part at once: you divide and conquer, and you move systematically, gradually changing the program specification in English to the Turing program that solves the problem. Part way along in the process there will be some English and some Turing.

Many people advise you to use this method for every program you create. For simple programs it hardly seems necessary. But for larger programs it can be very helpful.

Here is a summary of what you do:

- Decide what the program is to accomplish.

- Work out detailed specifications for the form the input data is to take and the form in which you want the output data.

- The problem is: to transform the input data into the output data.

- Devise an algorithm for doing the transformation by the process of step-by-step refinement.

An Example of Step-by-Step Refinement

Here is a problem:

You are to get the computer to deal cards for the four hands in the game of bridge. Each hand is to contain 13 cards. There are 52 cards in a deck consisting of equal numbers of 4 suits: spades, hearts, diamonds, and clubs. The card values in each suit go from 1 to 13, that is: 1 for the ace, 11 for the jack, 12 for the queen, and 13 for the king.

The details of the input data are that we need a number of constants which are included in the program. We can write these out in Turing.

```
const cardsindeck := 52
const cardsinhand := 13
const numberofhands := 4
const numberofsuits := 4
const cardsinsuit := 13
const suit: array 1 .. 4 of string (1) :=
              init ("S", "H", "D", "C")
```

The form of the output data is to be a list of the cards in each hand, giving suit and value for each. We will not at this stage sort the hands, as you would do in a bridge game. The hands will be identified by numbers from 1 to 4. We could change the program later to sort the hands and display them the way they appear in any newspaper article on bridge with north, south, east, and west labelled and the dealer identified.

We must transform the input data into the output data. Here is our first attempt at describing the way we will do this. Most of the description at this stage will be in English

> Generate the deck of cards
>
> Shuffle the deck
>
> Deal four hands
>
> Output the hands

At this stage we see we will need some variables to hold the information we generate from the constants. For the card deck we will use an array of records defined this way

```
type cardType:
    record
        value: int
        suit: string (1)
    end record
var deck: array 1 .. cardsindeck of cardType
```

We also need a counter called *card* to index the array, so we include this declaration

```
var card: int
```

We will now try to refine the part *Generate the deck of cards*:

```
% Generate the deck of cards
card := 1
for whichsuit: 1 .. numberofsuits
    for whichvalue: 1 .. cardsinsuit
        deck (card).value := whichvalue
        deck (card).suit := suit (whichsuit)
        card := card + 1
    end for
end for
```

Next we must *Shuffle the deck*. To do this we must devise an algorithm. Here is one:

> For each card in deck in turn
>> Generate a random number between 1 and *cardsindeck*
>> Swap the card with the card the random number picks.

This can be refined now:

```
% For each card in deck in turn
randomize
var where: int
for whichcard: 1 .. cardsindeck
    % Generate random number between 1
    % and cardsindeck
    randint (where, 1, cardsindeck)
    (Swap the card with the one designated by where)
end for
```

We have to refine the part that is still in English:

```
% Swap the card with the one designated by where
var temp: cardType
temp := deck (whichcard)
deck (whichcard) := deck (where)
deck (where) := temp
```

Here is the program section for shuffling the deck:

```
% Shuffle the deck
% For each card in deck in turn
randomize
var where: int
var temp: cardType
for whichcard: 1 .. cardsindeck
    % Generate random number between 1
    % and cardsindeck
    randint (where, 1, cardsindeck)
    % Swap the card with one designated by where
    temp := deck (whichcard)
    deck (whichcard) := deck (where)
    deck (where) := temp
end for
```

Notice how convenient the record data type is for the swapping operation.

Now we must refine the part that is: *Deal four hands.*

We must set up variables for the hands. Each hand will contain 13 cards, each of which can be represented by a record. So the four hands could be represented by a table with 4 columns and 13 rows each element of which is a record.

Here is the declaration

```
var hand: array 1 .. numberofhands, 1 .. cardsinhand
              of cardType
```

We must now develop the algorithm for dealing the hands. Here it is:

```
% Deal four hands
% Count the cards from the shuffled deck
%  start at first
card := 1
% Deal one card to each hand in turn
for cardcount: 1 .. cardsinhand
    for handcount: 1 .. numberofhands
        hand (handcount,cardcount) := deck (card)
        % Move to next card in deck
        card := card + 1
    end for
end for
```

Now we must output the hands. This needs no refinement as it is just a matter of outputting a table a column at a time and is this:

```
% Output the hands
for whichhand: 1 .. numberofhands
    put "Here are the cards for hand ", whichhand
    for whichcard: 1 .. cardsinhand
        put hand (whichhand, whichcard).suit: 3,
            hand (whichhand, whichcard).value
    end for
end for
```

Procedures with Global Variables

In a problem like this, where we have developed four relatively separate parts to carry out the English description of the problem solution, we could make each part into a separate procedure. Each part uses the information about the constants defined at the beginning and the declaration of the card deck. If we tried to produce procedures with parameters, we would need to use a lot of parameters for each one. So we give up and use the fact that all things defined in the main program are known (global to) to all the subprograms. So, for example, by placing the heading

procedure generateDeck

in front of the instructions produced for this and ending with:

end generateDeck

we could create a parameterless procedure that used global variables.

We could do this with each of the others and produce: *shuffleDeck, dealHands, outputHands,* as well. The table *hand* must be declared in the main program because it is used by both the last two procedures.

The main program is just this:

```
(declarations of constants and variables)
(definition of procedures)
generateDeck
shuffleDeck
dealHands
outputHands
```

Unfinished Procedures

We could leave some procedures in our program unfinished and refine them later. For example, if we had not yet devised the procedure *shuffleDeck* we could substitute this in the definitions

```
procedure shuffleDeck
    put "At this stage the deck should be shuffled"
end shuffleDeck
```

We call this sort of procedure a **stub**. It has the appearance of a procedure but does not do what it is supposed to do. You could test the rest of the program with this stub in place. The result should be the same thing as if you dealt an unshuffled deck – one that you just opened for the first time.

Using stubs lets you test parts of a program before it is completely ready. Some procedures are essential. For example, you could not deal hands unless the deck had been generated.

Problems

1.   Using the program for producing hands, add a procedure to sort the hands into suits and descending values.

2.   In outputting hands it is usual to replace the values for the face cards by their names: A for 1 standing for Ace, Q for 12 standing for Queen, and so on. Write an output procedure for hands that does this.

3.   In listing the cards in a hand that has been sorted, it is customary to list each suit on a separate line with the cards in that suit listed in decreasing order of value. Ace has the highest value, then King, then Queen, and so on. Here is a sample listing for a hand:

```
C      A K 3
D      Q 10 2
H      9 7 5
S      K J 3 2
```

Modify your program to produce this output.

4.   We have used the alphabetic sequence for the suits: Clubs, Diamonds, Hearts, Spades, In fact the usual way to list them is in the order of S, H, D, C, the exact reverse of the alphabetic order. Could you modify the sorting program to do it that way.

5.   A long poem is stored on the disk in a file named "poem". Write a program to read the poem a line at a time and count the number of words in the line. Prepare a frequency distribution of words in the line for the poem and output it as a bar chart of asterisks. For example, if there are 12 lines containing 5 words each the line of the bar chart opposite 5 will contain 12 asterisks.

Questions for Discussion

1.   Why do people who pose problems not always give you complete specifications?

2.   Is the method used to shuffle the deck of cards in the program given in this chapter the only one that we could use? Could you think of another possible shuffling algorithm?

3.   Is it essential that you keep a record of your steps in the step-by-step refinement method?

4.   How can you use the computer as you develop a program and save the development at various stages?

5.   Why must global variables be used with great caution?

Technical Terms you should now know

step-by-step refinement   stub
stepwise refinement

Chapter 16

SEEKING BETTER SOLUTIONS

*It is only when seeking a better solution
would result in a significant payoff
that we bother to try.*

In our presentation of the systematic method of problem solving, one part of the process required us to:

Assess whether there are more efficient algorithms for producing the same result.

We explained that in many cases this is an unnecessary step in the process because an efficient solution does not make the computer run a great deal faster.

The reason it is unnecessary is that an efficient solution would not run on the computer that much faster that it made any difference.

But, if we could find methods that were very much better, particularly if the problem takes the computer a reasonably long time to solve, then it would be worthwhile. There would be a payoff for your efforts.

A better solution is only worthwhile if it provides a signficant payoff.

Questions and Answers on Program Efficiency

Q.   What do we mean when we say that one method of solution by computer is more efficient than another?

A.   The more efficient method does not take as much work.

Q.   How can you tell how much work a method takes?

A.   I could time it to see how long it took to execute.

Q.   Can you tell anything without actually running the program?

A.   I could make an estimate about the amount of work by reading the program.

Q.   If one method took 10 seconds to run and another took 12 seconds, which is the better method?

A.   The second is better but it is not really a significant improvement. It would not make much difference which method I used.

Q.   What do you call a significant improvement?

A.   Twice as fast would seem worthwhile.

Q.   What do you call an improvement that is 10 times as fast?

A.   You got me.

Q.   We say it is **an order of magnitude** better (that means 10 times better.)

Solutions that are Very Much Better

We have described a method for looking up a friend's phone number in a list. The method was to start at the beginning of the list and look at the names one after the other until the name is found or you come to the end of the list. If you come to the end of the list without finding it you say it is "unlisted" (at least it is not in your list).

To find a number in a list of N names and numbers you would, on the average, have to examine $N/2$ names. The average would be greater than that if you looked for many names that were unlisted. For every unlisted name, you would have to look at N names before you could be sure it was unlisted.

Looking at names sequentially, one after the other, in a list is called a **linear search**. For a small list of up to 50 names it is a reasonable method to use. But imagine trying to look up a number in the phone book for a large city with millions of names by that method. We definitely use a different method. But what is it?

We usually open a book at the place where we think we will find the name. We then look at a name at the top of one of the pages. If the name we want is alphabetically less than that, we look in the book between where it is open and the beginning. Otherwise we look at the other "half" of the book. By examining just one name we have cut the **search space** in half.

Having made such progress with the technique we repeat it, and, look next at the half-way point of the half you know the name must be in (provided it is listed). We make a second examination and then do it again – cutting the search space in half once more. We keep doing this until we are down to one number. Then that number is either the one we want, or the number is unlisted.

Let us see how efficient this method can be. If you had 1000 names and numbers, here is a table of the number of examinations done and the size of the remaining search space. We will work it out for 1024 names which might take more examination than for 1000 names, certainly not fewer.

Number of examinations	Number still left
1	512
2	256
3	128
4	64
5	32
6	16
7	8
8	4
9	2
10	1

It took 10 examinations to find the number in this list. By the linear search it would have taken 500 on the average. Certainly this is significantly more efficient. The method is called **binary search**, because on each examination the search space (list yet to be examined) is divided by 2.

For a short list of 32 names, the linear search takes an average of 16 examinations. By looking at the table for the binary search you can see that it takes 5 examinations to narrow it down from 32 to one name. The difference in efficiency is not nearly as significant.

The catch to using binary search is that the list must be sorted.

Binary Search: A Better Solution

We will now develop a program for a binary search using the step-by-step refinement method. Here is a first step in the refinement

```
Initialize binary search
Search until one element left
loop
    Find the middle of the list
    if name sought >= entry at middle then
        Discard first half including the middle
    else
```

```
        Discard last half after middle
    end if
    exit when only one name left
end loop
```

We will program this as a procedure that will accept a list of records of type *listType* given by this declaration.

```
type listType:
    record
        name: string (40)
        phone: string (8)
    end record
```

Here it is:

```
procedure binSearch (phoneFile: array 1 .. * of
            listType, var friend: string (*),
            count: int, var place: int)
    var first, last, middle: int
    if length (friend) <= 40 then
        % Pad with blanks
        friend := friend +
            repeat (" ", 40 – length (friend))
    end if
    % Initialize binary search
    first := 1
    last := count
    % Search until one element left
    loop
        % Find the middle of the list
        middle := (first + last) div 2
        if friend >= phoneFile (middle).name then
            % Discard first half
            % including the middle
            first := middle + 1
        else
            % Discard last half after middle
            last := middle
        end if
```

```
            exit when first >= last
        end loop
        if phoneFile (first).name = friend then
            place := first
        else
            place := 0
        end if
    end binSearch
```

Better Solutions for Sorting

We have seen that searching in longer lists can be made very much more efficient if the list is sorted. This means that sorting a list will be an operation that is essential to efficiency. The sorting itself must be done efficiently. We have shown two methods of sorting so far: sorting by selection and successive merge sorting. The second method is much more efficient, although somewhat more difficult to understand.

We will look first at a way to improve the efficiency of the selection method we used. If you remember, we had two arrays one containing the unsorted list and the second for storing the elements that we select one-by-one to go in the sorted list. As each element was selected, we destroyed it in the original list as a possible candidate by overwriting the name with "zzz". To assess how much work this sorting method requires you note that, if the list has N elements, you must do $N-1$ examinations for each entry you select for the sorted list. So the total number of examinations you must do to sort the whole list is $N(N-1)$ since there are N elements to be selected.

We will now make a slight modification which will make an improvement. In the modification, you do not have a second array for the sorted list but as each element is selected you swap it with the one in the list that has its proper position in the final sorted list. We will do this with an example to show you what we mean. Instead of looking for the least each time, we will look for the greatest and move it to the end of the list. So instead of overwriting the original list with "zzz" you will only examine the list from the start to the point where you have the already sorted entries.

We will assume that we are sorting an array of records with names and telephone numbers as we had for the binary search.

```
procedure selectSort (
            var phoneFile: array 1 .. * of listType,
            count: int)
    % Declare temporary space for swapping
    var temp: listType
    var place : int
    var greatest: string (40)
    for decreasing j: count .. 1
        % Select largest of remaining j elements
        greatest := phoneFile (1).name
        place := 1
        for k: 2 .. j
            if greatest < phoneFile (k).name then
                greatest := phoneFile (k).name
                place := k
            end if
        end for
        % Swap element at place with element at j
        temp := phoneFile (j)
        phoneFile (j) := phoneFile (place)
        phoneFile (place) := temp
    end for
end selectSort
```

Now we will look at the efficiency of this modified selection sort. For the first select we must do $N-1$ examinations. For the next we only do $N-2$ examinations, and so on. The total of this series for N elements is

$$N(N-1) / 2$$

which is half the number of examinations required by our first method of selection. A small improvement.

If we use merging combined with selection we get a still better result. Suppose you have a list of N elements. You divide this into two lists each of $N/2$ elements. Then sorting each half by selection requires (using our better selection method):

$$(N/2)\ (N/2-1)\ /\ 2$$

For both halves we need twice this, namely:

$$N/2\ (N/2-1)$$

which is

$$\frac{N^2}{4} - \frac{N}{2}$$

To merge two lists requires one examination for every item in the merged list, so we must add to this N examinations. This makes a total of

$$\frac{N^2}{4} + \frac{N}{2}$$

Comparing this to the straight selection method which gave

$$\frac{N^2}{2} - \frac{N}{2}$$

we see that the select-merge method takes only about one half the number of examinations for large N. (Note if N is large the value of N^2 is much greater than N). For select-merge the number is approximately $N^2/4$ where it is $N^2/2$ for the straight selection.

You can imagine for yourself that the successive merge sort we did earlier is probably much more efficient still.

Problems

1.   Another method of sorting that we have not mentioned is **insertion sorting**. This requires two arrays. As each element of the unsorted list is examined in turn, it is placed in its proper place in the sorted list. This means it is inserted where it belongs, relative to the ones already there. Some elements already in the sorted list must be moved to make room, unless the new element happens to go at the end. Try programming an insertion sort.

2.   Is an insertion sort more or less efficient than a selection sort? Estimate the number of examinations required. What about the movement that is required as each element is inserted?

3.   Create some artificial data and compare linear search and binary search experimentally.

Questions for Discussion

1. We want to decide to make programs more efficient if they are to be used frequently. How does this correspond to what is known in economics as "cost-benefit analysis"?

2. Binary search is so much more efficient than linear search for a large file that most files are kept in a sorted order. How do we balance the relative costs of sorting and searching in a cost-benefit analysis?

3. Could you list the various methods of sorting discussed in this text. Other good methods are *Shellsort* and *Quicksort*. Could you find out about these from other books?

4. How is it that we can estimate relative efficiency of different algorithms without any reference to what kind of computer they will be run on?

Technical Terms you should now know

linear search
binary search
search space

efficiency of method
insertion sort

Chapter 17

PROBLEMS THAT COMPUTERS CAN NOT SOLVE

. . . the field of artificial intelligence. . .
is still in its infancy . . . there is not yet
any proof that what is being attempted
cannot be accomplished.

We have emphasized that computers do not, in fact, solve problems but that you can use computers to help you solve problems.

This is done by developing an algorithm for solving the problem and expressing it in a programming language such as Turing.

In this chapter we will look at two cases where we know for certain that you cannot solve the problem. The first is where the time required to carry out the solution on the computer becomes hopelessly long. The second is where there is an **ethical judgment** involved – a judgment that can not be reduced to an algorithm.

There are an enormous number of problems that computers can not at present solve, problems that are being looked at in the computer science field of **artificial intelligence**. This field is still in its infancy and, although progress is slow, there is not yet any proof that what is being attempted cannot be accomplished.

Questions and Answers about Insoluble Problems

Q.   What reason could there be for a problem to be unsolvable?

A.   When the specifications have contradictory requirements. For example, when you try to settle the time for a meeting that everyone must attend and there is no free hour in the whole week when everyone is available.

Q.   What do you do in a case like this?

A.   You decide to have the meeting when there will be as few absences as possible.

Q.   You make a judgment between having a few people away or having no meeting at all and chose the former. What do you call such a judgment?

A.   A **value judgment**.

Q.   Can computers make value judgments?

A.   No, you do, but you could program an algorithm that incorporated your value judgment.

Q.   Let's change the subject. Can you imagine an algorithm that can be programmed but that will not give a result?

A.   Perhaps one that just took forever to execute. The answer would never come out.

Computational Complexity

In the chapter on better solutions we compared two methods of searching: the linear search and the binary search. The binary search was much more efficient. But, even if you used the linear search, the time was reasonable. It was proportional to the number items N in the list.

The selection method is a reasonable method for sorting, but a successive merge sort is more efficient. With selection the time was proportional to $N(N - 1)$, or $N^2 - N$. Both this time and the one for linear search, is proportional to a **polynomial** in N. Any problem that can be solved in **polynomial time** obviously can be solved on a computer if N is not too large.

But there are other problems for which the time is not polynomial but might be, for example, **exponential**. If the time to deal with N items in a problem was, say proportional to

$$2^N$$

then as N becomes large the time grows exponentially. (The N is the exponent.) For this kind of problem there is no practical solution; it just takes too long to calculate.

We measure the **computational complexity** of any problem by looking at these expressions for the length of execution time. A large number of problems are of this kind that are hopelessly long to compute for any but the simplest case.

A famous example is the travelling salesperson problem, where there are a number of cities to be visited and a cost to go between each two cities (that have a connection). You are to find a trip for the salesperson that has the person go once (and only once) to each city and has a minimum cost for the trip. Sounds easy enough but it is one of the "hopeless" problems.

Getting Approximate Solutions

Since no algorithm has ever been found that is of the "good" polynomial kind for solving problems like the travelling salesperson problem, we must resort to methods that are second best.

What we do is try to find a routing that has a reasonably small cost, perhaps not the minimum, but one you could live with. To do this we try various techniques for guessing. A guessing principle is called an **heuristic principle**.

For example, in the salesperson problem we guess that wherever we are in the salesperson's tour we will choose the city next that is the cheapest to get to and which we have not yet visited. We may have to **backtrack** in this solution technique because we may arrive at a city and have nowhere to go from it that we have not yet been.

We do not suggest that this is a practical heuristic to use, but it illustrates the idea of inventing a guessing principle as a means to getting an approximate solution. This act of invention requires creative thinking. It is not straight logic. It requires imagination.

Making Use of Problems that are Hard to Solve

Another problem that is not, as far as we know, solvable by a polynomial time algorithm is to find what two prime numbers have been multiplied together to produce a rather large product. You are given the product and asked to find its two **prime factors**. For example, for the product 391 the prime factors are 17 and 23.

This particular "hard" problem is the basis of a system for scrambling (**encrypting**) digital messages that are to be transmitted so that they can not be understood without the **key** to the encryption. It helps to ensure privacy of data transmission.

Ethical Problems

We have included in problems that computers can not solve ones involving judgment about values such as which course of action is: good, better, best. Other judgments that we think of as ethical (or moral) are about: right and wrong; justice and injustice; and fair and unfair. Then there are ones that are legal or illegal.

Some of these judgments follow definite rules, just as mathematics has rules, and you know when a correct solution to a problem is given. But rules may vary from one group of people to another.

We must each develop our own **value systems** usually based on the experience of others but on our own as well. When a solution is arrived at based on a value system it should be identified as such. It is a personal solution not a general solution such as those for a logical or mathematical problem.

Ethical Problems about Computers

Every new technology brings its problems. No matter how beneficial it seems at first there is always a dark side. For example, the green revolution: to improve the harvest from farms by using pesticides and chemical fertilizers. Another is the use of nuclear reactors as energy sources. Computers too generate problems, as well as solving them. Here are some of the problems:

* *In keeping data banks of records about people.* Who is to have access to the information in the record: only the agency that collects the information, the person about whom the information is collected, anyone else who asks for or possibly pays for the information? Here there are issues of **privacy** and of **freedom of information**. There must be developed rules about many kinds of information: medical records, police records, income tax records, and financial records such as credit card data

- *In industries and business that use computers.* Are the computers used to maintain surveillance on the employees by monitoring productivity? Is the quality of the job improved or made worse because computers are used? Are computers causing unemployment or are they improving the chances of greater economic health and benefit to all? Is a higher educational standard becoming necessary because jobs require it?

- *In education and government.* Are computers enhancing the rights and opportunities for individuals or are they subjecting them to greater control and homogenization? Are computers in schools improving true education? Do computers in defense increase the chance of wars and subsequent disaster? Do computers in the stock market used for program trading cause crashes? Are the rights of individuals eroded as greater computer control is exercised?

There are many more questions than answers. Clearly we must all be alert to the perils. But just because there is a dark side to computers there is no need to give them up. In fact, like it or not, we are unlikely to turn back the clock to the days without them. We must see that we are the ones who control them and not they (or the people who use them) who control us.

Behaving Ethically about Computers

Since often the computers that we use are owned by someone else or shared with someone else we should always respect them and not damage them.

Computer software is easily copied just as the pages of a book are copied by a photocopier. You probably can tell from this book about problem solving and computing that good software requires a lot of human effort. The person or persons making that effort have a right to be paid for their work. This right is expressed in the fact that almost all software is **copyright**. It really belongs to the maker. We pay for a copy and can use the copy we paid for only according to the agreement we undertook when we bought it.

Schools or business buy copies of software for the use of students in school or employees at work. Copying software for home use is **illegal**. Of course, if you need it, the software could be bought for personal or home use just as it is for school or business.

Sometimes by paying a fee to the software producer the right to make a certain number of copies is granted. Make sure before you are guilty of theft. Your behavior should be guided by ethical principles, not by the likelihood of being caught in an unethical act.

- Crimes are sometimes committed by people with access to computer systems. These may be financial, where employees arrange to transfer company funds for their own use. They may be mischievous, where computers are invaded by outsiders through network access. Interfering with the data or programs belonging to someone else is a crime. Some hackers think it is a sign of prowess to cause trouble or simply make a joke. It is a punishable offense.

Artificial Intelligence

When computers first appeared in numbers in the early 1950s they were dubbed "mechanical brains". They could do arithmetic – an activity formerly done by people. It was **mental work**. These were in contrast to machines used in factories that did **physical work**.

Many researchers had unlimited ambitions for computers: to translate languages, prove theorems, or solve problems in general.

Demonstrations were often based on getting computers to play games. These were simple at first like Xs and Os (tic-tac-toe). The machine never lost a game against a human opponent. It tied many. There is an algorithm for play which we could learn too.

Next came checkers, then chess. To decide on a move in chess, the machine explores a **tree of possibilities** at each position and choses the "best" move by a heuristic method. The tree of possibilities grows exponentially and can not be calculated to the end.

Present day computer chess programs are expert at the game and can be bought at many stores. They let you play with a computer opponent of a variety of levels of skill. The "better" player takes longer to make each move.

Present day activity in artificial intelligence is concentrating on how to represent knowledge and use it in a system. **Expert systems** use a very limited **knowledge base**. The program must be able to make **inferences**, to work out a series of steps to arrive at a reasoned answer.

These expert systems have been used for diagnosis for medical purposes, geological exploration, or automobile repair. They must be used by human experts as an aid since the computer's expertise can not yet be thought of as independently reliable.

Other areas of AI involve understanding natural language, computer vision, theorem proving, machine learning, and robotics. Coupled with AI is the area of understanding human thinking and learning – the area of **cognitive science**.

Questions for Discussion

1.   The problem is to pack parcels of various sizes into a knapsack of given capacity so that there is a minimum amount of space wasted in the knapsack. Does this sound like a problem that is unsolvable in a reasonable time? Why?

2.   Could a computer program carry out your value judgments?

3.   Do you use any heuristic principles in playing games to win? Consider any of baseball, hockey, blackjack, bridge, or others.

4.   Why is finding the factors of a product of two prime numbers so difficult?

5.   Why would we want personal information to be private?

6.   Why should you be able to see records pertaining to yourself?

7.   Performance of people in jobs is always being evaluated for pay increases and promotions. What is bad about computer monitoring?

8.   Could you get too dependent on computers for your own good?

9.   What is program trading in the stock market?

10.   What harm does it do if you copy software for your own use?

11.   What is a computer virus? Is it a crime to originate a virus?

12.   What is the algorithm for never losing at *Xs* and *Os*?

13.   Why is understanding natural language so difficult?

14.   Do you know of any expert system?

Technical Terms you should now know

artificial intelligence	privacy
ethical judgment	freedom of information
value judgment	copyright
computational complexity	tree of possibilities
polynomial time	expert system
exponential algorithm	inference
heuristic principle	knowledge representation
prime factor	knowledge base
encryption of data	cognitive science
value system	

Appendix 1:

SIMPLIFIED SYNTAX OF TURING

To describe any language you must know its grammar or **syntax**. The following is a simplified version of the syntax of the Turing programming language. For a full Turing syntax see the textbook *Introduction to Computer Science using the Turing Programming Language* by J.N.P. Hume and R.C. Holt published by HSA Inc.

The syntax given here has been simplified in several ways. A number of the advanced features of the Turing language have not been discussed in this book. These have been omitted from this syntax. The syntax description given here is a formal description and many seem somewhat strange to you. But here it is:

- Turing programs are constructed by applying the **production rules** given here.

- Each production rule defines a **syntactic variable** such as a *program* in terms of other syntactic variables and strings of characters (tokens) that will ultimately form part of the Turing program.

- For example, the first production rule listed is

    A *program* is:
    > {declarationOrStatementInMainProgram}

    The syntactic variable *program* is defined in terms of another syntactic variable. called *declarationOrStatementInMainProgram*. Around this variable's name are curly braces which mean that this variable can occur zero or more times in a *program*.

- To **produce** a Turing program we would begin by looking at the production rule for *declarationOrStatementInMainProgram* and substitute for it.

- When you have a rule which produces a word in boldface type you have produced part of the final program and no more production rules can be applied to that part. It is a **terminal** token.

- The syntactic variables are called non-terminals and you must continue to replace them by their definition.

- In these syntax rules all the terminals are keywords in the Turing language.

- In a program you must replace the syntactic variable *id*, which stands for identifier, by a word you invent which follows the rules for identifiers listed under "Identifiers and Explicit Constants" given at the end of the syntax. Such words are terminal tokens but are not keywords in the language.

- In production rules anything enclosed in square brackets [ ] is optional. Anything in curly braces { } can occur zero or more times. To summarize:

    [item] means that item is optional, and
    {item} means that item can occur zero or more times.

Programs and Declarations

A *program* is:
        {*declarationOrStatementInMainProgram*}

A *declarationOrStatementInMainProgram* is one of:
       a.   *declaration*
       b.   *statement*
       c.   *subprogramDeclaration*

A *declaration* is one of the following:
    a.   *constantDeclaration*
    b.   *variableDeclaration*
    c.   *typeDeclaration*

A *constantDeclaration* is one of:
    a.   **const** *id* := *expn*
    b.   **const** *id* [: *typeSpec*]:= *initializingValue*

An *initializingValue* is one of:
    a.   *expn*
    b.   **init**(*initializingValue* {, *initializingValue*})
A *variableDeclaration* is one of:
    a.   **var** *id* {, *id* } := *expn*
    b.   **var** *id* {, *id* } : *typeSpec* [:= *initializingValue*]

Types

A *typeDeclaration* is:
    type *id* : *typeSpec*

A *typeSpec* is one of the following:
    a.   *standardType*
    b.   *subrangeType*
    c.   *arrayType*
    d.   *recordType*
    e.   *namedType*

A *standardType* is one of:
    a.   **int**
    b.   **real**
    c.   **boolean**
    d.   **string** [(*compileTimeExpn*)]

A *subrangeType* is:
> *compileTimeExpn .. expn*

An *arrayType* is:
> **array** *indexType* {, *indexType* } **of** *typeSpec*

An *indexType* is one of:
> a.   *subrangeType*
> b.   *namedType*

A *recordType* is:
> **record**
>> *id* {, *id* } : *typeSpec*
>> {*id* {, *id* } : *typeSpec* }
>
> **end record**

A *namedType* is:
> *id*

Subprograms

A *subprogramDeclaration* is:
> *subprogramHeader*
> *subprogramBody*

A *subprogramHeader* is one of:
> a.   **procedure** *id* [(*parameterDeclaration*
>> {, *parameterDeclaration* })]
>
> b.   **function** *id* [(*parameterDeclaration*
>> {, *parameterDeclaration* })] : *typeSpec*

A *parameterDeclaration* is:
> [**var**] *id* {, *id* } : *parameterType*

A parameterType is one of:

    a.   *typeSpec*

    b.   **string** (*)

    c.   **array** *compileTimeExpn ..* * {, *compileTimeExpn ..*}
           of *typeSpec*

    d.   **array** *compileTimeExpn ..* * {, *compileTimeExpn ..* * }
           of string (*)

A subprogramBody is:

        declarationsAndStatements

    end *id*

Statements and Input/Output

DeclarationsAndStatements is:

        {*declarationOrStatement* }

A declarationOrStatement is one of:

    a.   *declaration*

    b.   *statement*

A statement is one of the following:

    a.   *variableReference* := *expn*

    b.   *procedureCall*

    c.   **assert** *booleanExpn*

    d.   **result** *expn*

    e.   *ifStatement*

    f.   *loopStatement*

    g.   **exit** [**when** *booleanExpn*]

    h.   *caseStatement*

    i.   *forStatement*

    j.   *putStatement*

    k.   *getStatement*

    l.   *openStatement*

    m.   *closeStatement*

A *procedureCall* is a:
>   *reference*

An *ifStatement* is:
>   **if** *booleanExpn* **then**
>   *declarationsAndStatements*
>   {**elsif** *booleanExpn* **then**
>   *declarationsAndStatements* }
>   [**else**
>   *declarationsAndStatements*]
>   **end if**

A *loopStatement* is:
>   **loop**
>   *declarationsAndStatements*
>   **end loop**

A *caseStatement* is:
>   **case** *expn* **of**
>   **label** *compileTimeExpn* {, *compileTimeExpn* } :
>   *declarationsAndStatements*
>   {**label** *compileTimeExpn* {, *compileTimeExpn* } :
>   *declarationsAndStatements*}
>   [**label** : *declarationsAndStatements*]
>   **end case**

A *forStatement* is one of:
>   a.   **for** *id* : *forRange*
>   *declarationsAndStatements*
>   **end for**
>   b.   **for decreasing** *id* : *expn* .. *expn*
>   *declarationsAndStatements*
>   **end for**

The *id* may be omitted but is then not accessible.

A *forRange* is:
>   a.   *expn* .. *expn*

A *putStatement* is:
    put [: *streamNumber* ,] *putItem* {, *putItem* } [..]

A *putItem* is one of:
    a.   *expn* [: *widthExpn* [: *fractionWidth* [:
                               exponentWidth]]]
    b.   **skip**

A *getStatement* is:
    get [: *streamNumber* ,] *getItem* {, *getItem* }

A *getItem* is one of:
    a.   *variableReference*
    b.   **skip**
    c.   *variableReference* : *
    d.   *variableReference* : *widthExpn*

An *openStatement* is:
    open: *fileNumberVariable, fileName,*
                       capability {, *capability* }

A *capability* is one of:
    a.   **get**
    b.   **put**

A *closeStatement* is:
    close: *fileNumber*

A *streamNumber, widthExpn, fractionWidth, exponentWidth* , or *fileNumber* is an:
    expn

References and Expressions

A *variableReference* is a:
>   reference

A *reference* is one of:
>   a.   *id*
>   b.   *reference componentSelector*

A *componentSelector* is one of:
>   a.   (*expn* {, *expn* })
>   b.   . *id*

A *booleanExpn* or *compileTimeExpn* is an:
>   *expn*

An *expn* is one of the following:
>   a.   *reference*
>   b.   *explicitConstant*
>   c.   *substring*
>   d.   *expn infixOperator expn*
>   e.   *prefixOperator expn*
>   f.   (*expn*)

An *explicitConstant* is one of:
>   a.   *explicitUnsignedIntegerConstant*
>   b.   *explicitUnsignedRealConstant*
>   c.   *explicitStringConstant*
>   d.   **true**
>   e.   **false**

An *infixOperator* is one of:

a.   +   (integer and real addition; string concatenation)

b.   –   (integer and real subtraction;

c.   *   (integer and real multiplication)

d.   /   (real division)

e.   **div** (truncating integer division)

f.   **mod**   (integer remainder)

g.   **   (integer and real exponentation)

h.   <   (less than)

i.   >   (greater than)

j.   =   (equal to)

k.   <=   (less than or equal to)

l.   >=   (greater than or equal to)

m.   **not=**   (not equal)

n.   **and**   (boolean and)

o.   **or**   (boolean inclusive or)

A *prefixOperator* is one of:

a.   +   (integer and real identity)

b.   –   (integer and real negation)

c.   **not**   (boolean negation)

All infix operators (including **) associate left-to-right. The precedence of all the operators is as follows, in decreasing order of precedence (tightest binding to loosest binding):

1.   **

2.   prefix +, −

3.   *, /, **div**, **mod**

4.   infix +,−

5.   <, >, =, <=, >=, **not=**

6.   **not**

7.   **and**

8.   **or**

A *substring* is:

       reference (substringPosition [.. substringPosition])

A *substringPosition* is one of:

    a.   *expn*

    b.   ** [– expn]*

Identifiers and Explicit Constants

An *identifier* consists of a sequence of at most 50 letters, digits, and underscores beginning with a letter. All these characters are significant in distinguishing identifiers. Upper and lower case letters are considered to be distinct in identifiers and keywords; hence *j* and *J* are different identifiers. The keywords must be in lower case. Keywords and predefined identifiers must not be redeclared (they are reserved words).

An *explicit string constant* is a sequence of zero or more characters surrounded by double quotes. Within explicit string constants, the back slash character (\) is an escape to represent certain characters as follows: \" for double quote, \n or \N for end of line character, \t or \T for tab, \f or \F for form feed, \r or \R for return, \b or \B for backspace, \e or \E for escape, \d or \D for delete, and \\ for back slash. Explicit string constants must not cross line boundaries.

Character values are ordered by the ASCII collating sequence.

An *explicit integer constant* is a sequence of one or more decimal digits, optionally preceded by a plus or minus sign.

An *explicit real constant* consists of three parts: an optional plus or minus sign, a *significant figures part,* and an *exponent part*. The significant figures part consists of a sequence of one or more digits optionally containing a decimal point. The exponent part consists of the letter *e* (or *E*) followed optionally by a plus or minus sign followed by one or more digits. If the significant figures part contains a decimal point then the exponent part is optional. The following are examples of explicit real constants.

      2.0   0.   .1   2e4   –56.1e+27

An explicit integer or real constant that begins with a sign is called a *signed* constant; without the sign, it is called an *unsigned* constant.

The explicit boolean constants are **true** and **false**.

Appendix 2:

PREDEFINED SUBPROGRAMS

Predefined Functions

eof (i: **int**): **boolean**

Accepts a non-negative stream number (see description of **get** and **put** statements) and returns true if, and only if, there are no more characters in the stream. This function must not be applied to streams that are being written to (via **put**). The parameter and parentheses can be omitted, in which case it is taken to be the default input stream.

length (s : **string**): **int**

Returns the number of characters in the string. The string must be initialized.

index (s , patt : **string**): **int**

If there exists an i such that $s(i .. i + length(patt) - 1) = patt$, then the smallest such i is returned, otherwise zero is returned. Note that 1 is returned if patt is the null string.

repeat (s : **string**, i : **int**): **string**

If $i > 0$, returns i copies of s joined together, else returns the null string. Note that if $j \geq 0$, $length(repeat(t, j)) = j * length(t)$.

hasch : **boolean**

Value is true if single character has been read by procedure getch.

playdone : **boolean**

Value is true if the execution of the preceding play procedure is finished.

whatcolor : **int**

Value is the current color number in which characters will be displayed in pixel graphics.

whatcolorback : **int**

> Value is the current background color number in pixel graphics.

maxx : **int**

> Maximum value of x in current pixel graphics mode. For CGA, *maxx* = 319.

maxy : **int**

> Maximum value of y in current pixel graphics mode. For CGA, *maxx* = 199.

maxcolor : **int**

> Value is the maximum color number in current pixel (or character) graphics mode. For CGA graphics, *maxcolor* = 3. For character graphics, *maxcolor* = 15.

Mathematical Functions

abs (*expn*)

> Accepts an integer or real value and returns the absolute value. The type of the result is **int** if the *expn* is of root type **int**, otherwise it is real.

max (*expn* , *expn*)

> Accepts two numeric (real or integer) values and returns their maximum. If both are of root type **int**, the result is an **int**; otherwise it is real.

min (*expn*, *expn*)

> Accepts two numeric (real or integer) values and returns their minimum. If both are of root type **int**, the result is an **int**; otherwise it is real.

sign (*r* : **real**): −1 .. 1

> Returns −1 if $r < 0$, 0 if $r = 0$, and 1 if $r > 0$.

sqrt (*r* : **real**): **real**

> Returns the positive square root of r, where r is a non-negative value.

sin (*r* : **real**): **real**

Returns the sine of *r*, where *r* is an angle expressed in radians.

cos (*r* : real): real

Returns the cosine of *r*, where *r* is an angle expressed in radians.

arctan (*r* : real): real

Returns the arctangent (in radians) of *r*.

sind (*r* : **real**): **real**

Returns the sine of *r*, where *r* is an angle expressed in degrees.

cosd (*r* : **real**): **real**

Returns the cosine of *r*, where *r* is an angle expressed in degrees.

arctand (*r* : **real**): **real**

Returns the arctangent (in degrees) of *r*.

ln (*r* : **real**): **real**

Returns the natural logarithm (base e) of *r*.

exp (*r* : **real**): **real**

Returns the natural base *e* raised to the power *r*.

Type Transfer Functions

floor (*r* : **real**): **int**

Returns the largest integer less than or equal to *r*.

ceil (*r* : **real**): **int**

Returns the smallest integer greater than or equal to *r*.

round (*r* : **real**): **int**

Returns the nearest integer approximation to *r*. Rounds to larger value in case of tie.

intreal (*i* : **int**): **real**

Returns the real value corresponding to *i*. No precision is lost in the conversion, so *floor*(*intreal*(*j*)) = *ceil*(*intreal*(*j*)) = *j*. To guarantee that these equalities hold, an implementation may limit the range of *i*..

chr (*i* : **int**): **string** (1)

Returns a string of length 1. The i-th character of the ASCII sequence is returned, where the first character corresponds to 0, the second to 1, etc. See ASCII code for characters. The selected character must not be *uninitchar* (a reserved character used to mark uninitialized strings) or *eos* (a reserved character used to mark the end of a string).

ord (*expn*)

Accepts a string of length 1 and returns the position of the   character in the ASCII sequence.

intstr (*i, width* : **int**): **string**

Returns a string equivalent to an integer *i*, padded on the left with blanks as necessary to a length of *width*; for example, *intstr* (14,4) = "ƀƀ14" where *b* represents a blank. The width parameter is optional. If it is omitted, it is taken to be 1. The width parameter must be non-negative. If width is not large enough to represent the value of *i*, the length is automatically increased as needed. The string returned by *intstr* is of the form:

$$\{blank\}[-]digit\{digits\}$$

The leftmost digit is non-zero, or else there is a single zero digit.

strint (*s*: **string**): **int**

Returns the integer equivalent to string *s*. String *s* must consist of a possibly null sequence of blanks, then an optional plus or minus sign, and finally a sequence of one or more digits. Note that for integer *i*, and for non-negative *w*, *strint*(*intstr*(*i, w*)) = *i*.

erealstr (*r.* **real**,*width, fractionWidth, exponentWidth* : **int**): **string**

Returns a string (including exponent) approximating *r*, padded on the left with blanks as necessary to a length of *width*; for example, *erealstr*(2.5e1,9,2,2) = "*b*2.50e+01" where *b* represents a blank. The *width* must be non-negative **int** value. If the *width* parameter is not large enough to represent the value of *r*, it is implicitly increased as needed. The *fractionWidth* parameter is the non-negative number of fractional digits to be displayed. The displayed value is rounded to the nearest decimal equivalent with this accuracy, with ties rounded to the next larger value. The *exponentWidth* parameter must be non-negative and gives the number of exponent digits to be displayed. If *exponentWidth* is not large enough to represent the exponent, more space is used as needed. The string returned by *erealstr* is of the form:

{blank}[−]digit,{digit}e sign digit {digit}

where "sign" is a plus or minus sign. The leftmost digit is non-zero, unless all the digits are zeroes.

frealstr (*r* : **real**, *width, fractionWidth*: **int**): **string**

Returns a string approximating *r*, padded on the left with blanks if necessary to a length of *width.* The number of digits of fraction to be displayed is given by *fractionWidth*; for example, *frealstr*(2.5e1,5,1) = "*b*25.0" where *b* represents a blank. The *width*must be non-negative. If the *width* parameter is not large enough to represent the value of *r*, it is implicitly increased as needed. The *fractionWidth* must be non-negative. The displayed value is rounded to the nearest decimal equivalent with this accuracy, with ties rounded to the next larger value. The result string is of the form:

{blank} [−] digit{digit}.{digit}

If the leftmost digit is zero, then it is the only digit to the left of the decimal point.

realstr (r : **real**, width : **int**): **string**

Returns a string approximating *r*, padded on the left with blanks if necessary to a length of *width*, for example, *realstr*(2.5e1,4) = "bb25" where *b* represents blank. The width parameter must be non-negative. If the *width* parameter is not large enough to represent the value of *r*, it is implicitly increased as needed. The displayed value is rounded to the nearest decimal equivalent with this accuracy, with ties rounded to the next larger value. The string *realstr*(*r*, *width*) is the same as the string *frealstr*(*r*, *width*, *defaultfw*) when *r* = 0 or when $1e-3 \leq abs(r) < 1e\ 6$, otherwise the same as *erealstr*(*r*, *width*, *defaultfw*, *defaultew*), with the following exceptions. With *realstr*, trailing fraction zeroes are omitted and if the entire fraction is zero, the decimal point is omitted. (These omissions take place even if the exponent part is output.) If an exponent is output, any plus sign and leading zeroes are omitted. Thus, whole number values are in general displayed as integers. *Defaultfw* is an implementation defined number of fractional digits to be displayed; for most implementations, *defaultfw* will be 6. *Defaultew* is an implementation defined number of exponent digits to be displayed; for most implementations, *defaultew* will be 2.

strreal (s : **string**): **real**

Returns a real approximation to string *s*. String *s* must consist of a possibly null sequence of blanks, then an optional plus or minus sign and finally an explicit unsigned real or integer constant.

Predefined Procedures

rand (**var** r : **real**)

Sets *r* to the next value of a sequence of pseudo random real numbers that approximates a uniform distribution over the range $0 < r < 1$.

randint (**var** i : int, low, high : **int**)

Sets *i* to the next value of a sequence of pseudo random integers that approximate a uniform distribution over the range $low \leq i$ and $i \leq high$. It is required that $low \leq high$.

randomize

This is a procedure with no parameters that resets the sequences of pseudo random numbers produced by *rand* and *randint*, so different executions of the same program will produce different results.

randnext (**var** *v* : **real**, *seq* : 1 .. 10)

This is the same as *rand*, except *seq*specifies one of 10 independent and repeatable sequences of pseudo random real numbers.

randseed (*seed* : **int**, *seq* : 1 .. 10)

This restarts one of the sequences generated by *randnext*. Each time this procedure is called with the same seed,*randnext* produces the same sequence of random number for the given *seq*.

The predefined procedures (*rand, randint, randomize, randnext,* and *(randseed)* have side effects. As a result, functions are not allowed to contain them or to directly or indirectly call procedures that contain them.

Graphics Procedures

locate (*row, column*: **int**)

Places the cursor at the point whose screen coordinates are (row, column). Valid values are $1 \leq row \leq 25$ and $1 \leq column \leq 80$.

cls

In character graphics mode, clears the screen and places cursor at point whose screen coordinates are (1, 1).

colorback (*colorNumber*: **int**)

Sets background color for characters to be displayed. Valid values for character graphics are $0 \leq colorNumber \leq 7$.

getch (**var** *character*: **string**(1))

Reads a single character from the keyboard.

play (music: **string**)

Plays notes according to the *music*. See details in music chapter.

setscreen (s : **string**)

Changes to mode designated by string *s*. If *s* is "graphics" changes to CGA pixel graphics mode. If *s* is "screen" changes to character graphics mode. If *s* is "text" changes to regular mode which is default mode.

cls

In pixel graphics mode, clears the screen and changes screen to current background color.

colorback (colorNumber : **int**)

Sets current background color. For CGA pixel graphics, the valid values are $0 \leq colorNumber \leq 15$. The default value is 0. The pixel color number 0 for all palette numbers has the color of current background. The default background color is black.

drawdot (x, y, color : **int**)

Sets a dot (pixel) of *color* at point (x, y).

drawline (x1, y1, x2, y2, color : **int**)

Draws a line in *color* from $(x1, y1)$ to $(x2, y2)$.

drawbox (x1, y1, x2, y2, color : **int**)

Draws a rectangle in *color* with sides parallel to the axes, bottom left corner at $(x1, y1)$, and upper right corner at $(x2, y2)$.

drawfillbox (x1, y1, x2, y2, color : **int**)

Draws a filled in rectangle in *color* with sides parallel to the axes, bottom left corner at $(x1, y1)$, and upper right corner at $(x2, y2)$.

drawoval (xCenter, yCenter, xRadius, yRadius, color : **int**)

Draws an oval in *color* with center at $(xCenter, yCenter)$, horizontal distance to oval *xRadius*, vertical distance *yRadius*.

drawfilloval (xCenter, yCenter, xRadius, yRadius, color : **int**)

Draws a filled in oval in *color* with center at $(xCenter, yCenter)$, horizontal distance to oval *xRadius*, vertical distance *yRadius*.

drawarc (xCenter, yCenter, xRadius, yRadius : **int**, initialAngle, finalAngle, color : **int**)

Draws a part of an oval whose specifications are given (as in *drawoval*) between two lines from the center that make angles in degrees: *initialAngle* and *finalAngle* , as measured counterclockwise from the three o'clock position as zero.

drawfillarc (xCenter, yCenter, xRadius, yRadius : **int**, initialAngle, finalAngle, color : **int**)

Draws a filled in "piece of pie" shaped wedge whose specifications are given (as in *drawoval*) between two lines from the center that make angles in degrees: *initialAngle* and *finalAngle*, as measured counterclockwise from the three o'clock position as zero.

drawfill (xInside, yInside, fillColor, borderColor : **int**)

Starting from a point (*xInside, yInside*) fills an area surrounded by *borderColor* with *fillColor* .

locatexy (x, y : **int**)

Changes the cursor position in pixel graphics (the cursor is not visible) to be in the nearest character position to point (*x, y*).

locate (row, column : **int**)

In pixel graphics sets to row and column position of text. In pixel graphics, the row and column position of text is the same as for character graphics, except that these are only 40 columns in row, not 80.

delay (duration : **int**)

Causes a delay of length *duration* milliseconds. A delay of duration 500 is half a second.

sound (frequency, duration : **int**)

Emits a sound of any *frequency* (cycles per second) for *duration* in milliseconds.

Appendix 3:

RESERVED WORDS IN TURING

Keywords

all	and	array	assert
begin	bind	body	boolean
by	case	close	collection
const	decreasing	div	else
elsif	end	enum	exit
export	external	false	fcn
for	forward	free	function
get	if	import	in
include	init	int	invariant
label	loop	mod	module
new	nil	not	of
opaque	open	or	pervasive
pointer	post	pre	proc
procedure	put	read	real
record	result	return	seek
set	skip	string	tag
tell	then	to	true
type	union	var	when
write			

Predefined Identifiers

abs	arctan	arctand	ceil
chr	clock	close	cls
color	colorback	colour	colourback
cos	cosd	date	delay
drawarc	drawbox	drawdot	drawfill
drawfillarc	drawfillbox	drawfilloval	drawfillpolygon
drawline	drawoval	drawpic	drawpolygon
eof	erealstr	exp	fetcharg
floor	frealstr	getch	getenv
getpid	hasch	index	intreal
intstr	length	ln	locate
locatexy	lower	max	maxcol
maxcolor	maxcolour	maxrow	maxx
maxy	min	nargs	nil
open	ord	palette	play
playdone	pred	rand	randint
randnext	randomize	randseed	realstr
repeat	round	screen	setscreen
sign	sin	sind	sizepic
sound	sqrt	strint	strreal
succ	sysclock	system	takepic
time	upper	wallclock	

whatcolorback   whatcolourback
whatcolor   whatcolour
whatdotcolor   whatdotcolour
whatpalette   whattextchar
whattextcolor   whattextcolour
whattextcolorback   whattextcolourback

Appendix 4:

COLORS IN TURING

IBM PC

Text or Screen Mode
Any 16 Color Graphics Mode

Color Number	Color	Color Number	Color
0	Black	8	Grey
1	Dark Blue	9	Blue
2	Dark Green	10	Green
3	Dark Cyan	11	Cyan
4	Dark Red	12	Red
5	Dark Magenta	13	Magenta
6	Brown	14	Yellow
7	White	15	Bright White

CGA Graphics Mode

Palette 0

Color Number	Color
0	Black
1	Dark Green
2	Dark Red
3	Brown

Palette 1

Color Number	Color
0	Black
1	Dark Cyan
2	Dark Magenta
3	White

Palette 2

Color Number	Color
0	Black
1	Green
2	Red
3	Yellow

Palette 3 [Default]

Color Number	Color
0	Black
1	Cyan
2	Magenta
3	Bright White

Macintosh

All Modes

Color Number	Color
0	White
1	Black

Icon

Graphics Mode 1

Color Number	Color
0	Black
1	White

Graphics Mode 2 and 4

Color Number	Color	Color Number	Color
0	Black	2	Green
1	Red	3	Bright White

Graphics Mode 3 and 5

Color Number	Color	Color Number	Color
0	Black	8	Dark Grey
1	Dark Red	9	Red
2	Dark Green	10	Green
3	Dark Yellow	11	Yellow
4	Dark Blue	12	Blue
5	Dark Magenta	13	Magenta
6	Dark Cyan	14	Cyan
7	Grey	15	White

Appendix 5:

IBM PC Keyboard Codes
The ASCII value of the character
returned by getch

	0	(space)	32	@	64	`	96
Ctrl-A	1	!	33	A	65	a	97
Ctrl-B	2	"	34	B	66	b	98
	3	#	35	C	67	c	99
Ctrl-D	4	$	36	D	68	d	100
Ctrl-E	5	%	37	E	69	e	101
Ctrl-F	6	&	38	F	70	f	102
Ctrl-G	7	'	39	G	71	g	103
Ctrl-H / BS	8	(	40	H	72	h	104
Ctrl-I / TAB	9	)	41	I	73	i	105
Ctrl-J / CR	10	*	42	J	74	j	106
Ctrl-K	11	+	43	K	75	k	107
Ctrl-L	12	,	44	L	76	l	108
Ctrl-M	13	-	45	M	77	m	109
Ctrl-N	14	.	46	N	78	n	110
Ctrl-O	15	/	47	O	79	o	111
Ctrl-P	16	0	48	P	80	p	112
Ctrl-Q	17	1	49	Q	81	q	113
Ctrl-R	18	2	50	R	82	r	114
Ctrl-S	19	3	51	S	83	s	115
Ctrl-T	20	4	52	T	84	t	116
Ctrl-U	21	5	53	U	85	u	117
Ctrl-V	22	6	54	V	86	v	118
Ctrl-W	23	7	55	W	87	w	119
Ctrl-X	24	8	56	X	88	x	120
Ctrl-Y	25	9	57	Y	89	y	121
Ctrl-Z	26	:	58	Z	90	z	122
Ctrl-[/ ESC	27	;	59	[	91	{	123
Ctrl-\	28	<	60	\	92	|	124
Ctrl-]	29	=	61	]	93	}	125
Ctrl-^	30	>	62	^	94	~	126
Ctrl-_	31	?	63	_	95	Ctrl-BS	127

Alt-9 128	Alt-D 160	F6 192	Ctrl-F3 224
Alt-0 129	Alt-F 161	F7 193	Ctrl-F4 225
Alt-- 130	Alt-G 162	F8 194	Ctrl-F5 226
Alt-= 131	Alt-H 163	F9 195	Ctrl-F6 227
Ctrl-PgUp 132	Alt-J 164	F10 196	Ctrl-F7 228
133	Alt-K 165	197	Ctrl-F8 229
134	Alt-L 166	198	Ctrl-F9 230
135	167	Home 199	Ctrl-F10 231
136	168	Up Arrow 200	Alt-F1 232
137	169	PgUp 201	Alt-F2 233
138	170	202	Alt-F3 234
139	171	Left Arrow 203	Alt-F4 235
140	Alt-Z 172	204	Alt-F5 236
141	Alt-X 173	Right Arrow 205	Alt-F6 237
142	Alt-C 174	206	Alt-F7 238
Back TAB 143	Alt-V 175	End 207	Alt-F8 239
Alt-Q 144	Alt-B 176	Down Arrow 208	Alt-F9 240
Alt-W 145	Alt-N 177	PgDn 209	Alt-F10 241
Alt-E 146	Alt-M 178	Ins 210	242
Alt-R 147	179	Del 211	Ctrl-L Arrow 243
Alt-T 148	180	Shift-F1 212	Ctrl-R Arrow 244
Alt-Y 149	181	Shift-F2 213	Ctrl-End 245
Alt-U 150	182	Shift-F3 214	Ctrl-PgDn 246
Alt-I 151	183	Shift-F4 215	Ctrl-Home 247
Alt-O 152	184	Shift-F5 216	Alt-1 248
Alt-P 153	185	Shift-F6 217	Alt-2 249
154	186	Shift-F7 218	Alt-3 250
155	F1 187	Shift-F8 219	Alt-4 251
156	F2 188	Shift-F9 220	Alt-5 252
157	F3 189	Shift-F10 221	Alt-6 253
Alt-A 158	F4 190	Ctrl-F1 222	Alt-7 254
Alt-S 159	F5 191	Ctrl-F2 223	Alt-8 255

Ctrl-@, Ctrl-C and Ctrl-Break will terminate a Turing
Program

Appendix 6:
Turing Character Set

0		32		64	@	96	`
1	☺	33	!	65	A	97	a
2	●	34	"	66	B	98	b
3	♥	35	#	67	C	99	c
4	◆	36	$	68	D	100	d
5	♣	37	%	69	E	101	e
6	not shown	38	&	70	F	102	f
7	·	39	'	71	G	103	g
8	not shown	40	(	72	H	104	h
9	not shown	41	)	73	I	105	i
10	not shown	42	*	74	J	106	j
11	not shown	43	+	75	K	107	k
12	not shown	44	,	76	L	108	l
13	not shown	45	-	77	M	109	m
14	♪	46	.	78	N	110	n
15	☼	47	/	79	O	111	o
16	►	48	0	80	P	112	p
17	◄	49	1	81	Q	113	q
18	↕	50	2	82	R	114	r
19	‼	51	3	83	S	115	s
20	¶	52	4	84	T	116	t
21	§	53	5	85	U	117	u
22	▬	54	6	86	V	118	v
23	↨	55	7	87	W	119	w
24	↑	56	8	88	X	120	x
25	↓	57	9	89	Y	121	y
26	→	58	:	90	Z	122	z
27	←	59	;	91	[	123	{
28	∟	60	<	92	\	124	|
29	↔	61	=	93	]	125	}
30	not shown	62	>	94	^	126	~
31	not shown	63	?	95	_	127	not shown

128	Ç	160	á	192	└	224	∝
129	ü	161	í	193	⊥	225	β
130	é	162	ó	194	┬	226	Γ
131	â	163	ú	195	├	227	π
132	ä	164	ñ	196	─	228	Σ
133	à	165	Ñ	197	┼	229	σ
134	å	166	ª	198	╞	230	µ
135	ç	167	º	199	╟	231	τ
136	ê	168	¿	200	╚	232	Φ
137	ë	169	⌐	201	╔	233	Θ
138	è	170	¬	202	╩	234	Ω
139	ï	171	½	203	╦	235	δ
140	î	172	¼	204	╠	236	∞
141	ì	173	¡	205	═	237	φ
142	Ä	174	«	206	╬	238	∈
143	Å	175	»	207	╧	239	∩
144	É	176	▒	208	╨	240	≡
145	æ	177	▓	209	╤	241	±
146	Æ	178	█	210	╥	242	≥
147	ô	179	│	211	╙	243	≤
148	ö	180	┤	212	╘	244	⌠
149	ò	181	╡	213	╒	245	⌡
150	û	182	╢	214	╓	246	÷
151	ù	183	╖	215	╫	247	≈
152	ÿ	184	╕	216	╪	248	°
153	Ö	185	╣	217	┘	249	·
154	Ü	186	║	218	┌	250	·
155	¢	187	╗	219	█	251	√
156	£	188	╝	220	▄	252	ⁿ
157	¥	189	╜	221	▌	253	²
158	₧	190	╛	222	▐	254	∎
159	ƒ	191	┐	223	▀	255	

Useful Characters for Drawing Lines

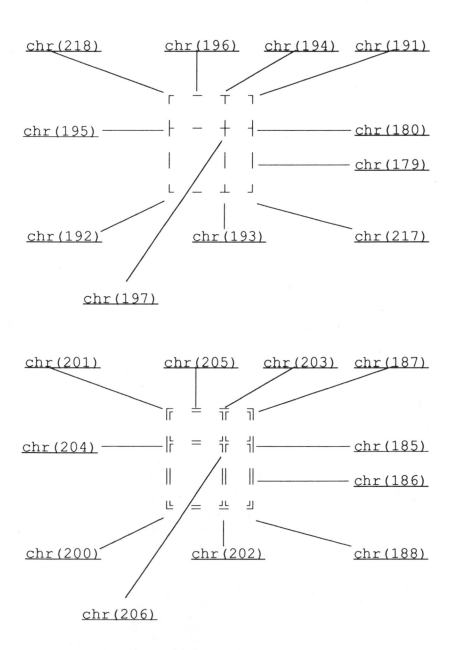

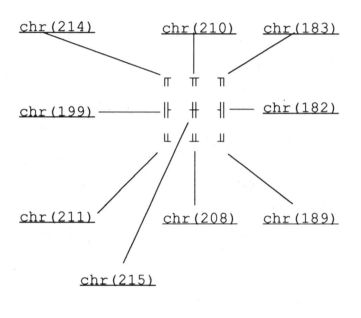

chr(214)   chr(210)   chr(183)

chr(199) ——————   —————— chr(182)

chr(211)   chr(208)   chr(189)

chr(215)

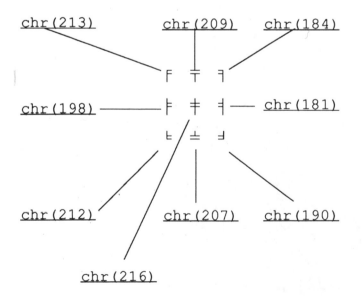

chr(213)   chr(209)   chr(184)

chr(198) ——————   —————— chr(181)

chr(212)   chr(207)   chr(190)

chr(216)

Appendix 7:

GLOSSARY OF TECHNICAL TERMS

Abstraction   the essence of an idea or object without details.

Active window   in a screen display system with several windows, the window that is currently referred to by menu selection, mouse pointing, or keyboard entry.

Actual parameter   the value or variable name that appears in parentheses after the name of a procedure or function when it is used in a program.

Algorithm   a step-by-step procedure by which certain results may be produced.

Analogy   describing one thing by reference to another. The earth is round like an orange is an analogy.

And   a logical operator connecting two conditions, each of which must be true if the compound condition is to be true.

Animation   achieving the effect of movement in a graphic by displaying a sequence of graphics, one after the other, with small changes from one to the next.

Annuity   a series of payments to be made annually.

Application program   computer software that can accomplish a particular function, such as one to process text or handle business accounting.

Arithmetic operator   symbol standing for operation of addition (+), subtraction (−), multiplication (*), or division (\).

Array   a group of variables that share a name and are distinguished from each other by each having a particular index value.

Arrow key   a key on the keyboard that causes the cursor to move in the direction of the arrow by one character space.

Artificial intelligence   the simulation on a computer of activities that are considered to require human intelligence.

ASCII code   a binary code chosen as the American Standard Code for Information Interchange.

Assertion   a statement in a program that causes an interruption in execution if the condition following the keyword **assert** is false.

Assignment statement   a statement that assigns a value to a variable.

Average   the value obtained by adding up the values of a number of items and dividing by that number.

Background color   the color filling a screen, or window, against which other colored symbols or objects can be displayed.

Backslash   the symbol \, used often as an escape character in a computer.

Backspace key   the key on the keyboard that causes the cursor to move back one space erasing the symbol it moves back over.

Basic   a programming language devised in the early days of interactive computing. It has undergone many modifications since and there are many incompatible dialects of Basic now in existence.

Binary form   a way of representing numerical values using only two digits, rather then the decimal form which uses ten digits.

Binary operation   a mathematical operation involving two values.

Binary search   searching for a particular item in a sorted list of items by successively dividing the list in two equal parts and discarding the half which cannot possibly contain the sought item. The process stops when only one item remains.

Bit   a binary digit.

Body of loop   the declarations and statements that are contained between the beginning of a loop and the end of the loop.

Boolean   variables that can have one of two values, true or false.

Brainstorming a method of working in a group to listen to a variety of suggestions about how to solve problems – the suggestions can be as "way out" as you like at this stage.

Byte a group of binary digits, often eight, that are treated as a unit.

Calculator a device for performing arithmetic operations.

Capital an upper case letter.

Case construct a program construct used for multi-way selection when the various alternatives are characterized by different integer values.

Case sensitive a language like Turing, that distinguishes between capital letters and little letters.

Cascaded selection a selection construct that contains one or more **elsif**s. It is used in multi-way selection.

CGA graphics one form of graphics system for PCs.

Character a symbol displayed on the screen or stored in the computer memory. It may be a letter, a digit, or a special symbol.

Character graphics obtaining a picture on the screen by the placement of character symbols in various rows and columns.

Clicking mouse pressing the button on the top of the mouse and releasing it quickly.

Clipboard a term used to refer to the buffer memory used to store any text that is deleted (or copied). Any subsequent deletion erases the current contents of the clipboard.

Closed figure a drawing that is continuous and ends at the same place that it starts.

Cognitive science the science of trying to understand the process of learning.

Color number the integer value that corresponds to a particular color that can be displayed.

Column   the spaces across the screen in which symbols can be displayed. Commonly there are 80 columns across a PC screen.

Color monitor   a screen capable of color displays.

Command   an instruction to the operating system of the computer.

Comment   a line (or part of a line) of a program that is used to identify it or describe what the program does in order to make it more understandable to someone reading it.

Commutative operation   a binary operation which results in the same value if the two operands are interchanged.

Comparison operator   an operator used in a condition to compare two values.

Compile-time error   a mistake in a program that can be discovered at the time the program is being translated before execution starts.

Compiling   translating a program in a high-level language into one that can be understood by a computer.

Computational complexity   a measure of the amount of calculation required to execute a particular algorithm.

Conditional loop   a repetition that is terminated when a particular condition holds.

Constant   a "variable" whose value never changes during the execution of a program.

Control-break   pressing the control and break keys simultaneously. This is often used to interrupt program execution.

Control structure   the sequence in which statements of a program are to be executed.

Coordinates   a specification of the position of a point on the screen.

Copyright   the ownership of rights and privileges to a particular intellectual property such as a book or computer software.

Correctness of a program   a program is correct if it produces the correct output for any possible input. Testing a program on a sample of possible inputs cannot prove correctness.

Counted loop   a repetition that is terminated when a counting index reaches a certain value. The index is altered by a fixed amount on each repetition.

Cursor   the symbol displayed on the screen that indicates where the next symbol input will be displayed.

Data   the information that is processed by a program.

Data base   a set of related pieces of information that is stored in the computer in a systematic way.

Data file on disk   a sequence of data items stored in secondary (disk) memory.

Data type   the kind of data represented, for example, numbers (real or integer) or strings of characters.

Debugging   looking for errors in a program and correcting them.

Decimal form   the usual way of representing numbers in the scale of ten.

Declaration of variable   a line in a program that causes memory to be reserved for the variable. The data type of the variable is given in the declaration since different types require different amounts of memory.

Desk top   a term used in a window system to show the files that are open or available.

Desk top publishing   using the computer (on your own desk) to create camera ready copy for printing.

Dialog box   a box which appears, usually in an operating system, and asks you to enter further information.

Digital computer   a computer that works on devices that have two states (say on or off) rather than one that represents information continuously as a light meter does.

Disk   a circular disk that can hold digital magnetic recordings and is used as a means of storing information on a long term basis.

Disk drive   the mechanism in the computer that spins the disk and has read and write heads for "playing" and recording.

Disk file name   each file on a disk must have a unique name by which it may be retrieved.

Directory of files   a list of the names of all files on disk that can be accessed at that time.

Documentation   descriptions in natural language and/or mathematics that help make programs understandable to the reader.

Drag   am operation with a mouse of pressing the button and holding it down as you move to another screen location.

Echo of input   when data is input from a keyboard it is usual for it to be displayed (or echoed) on the screen as it is being typed.

Edit   make changes in data or a program.

Editor   the systems program that allows you to enter and edit programs or data.

Efficiency of algorithm   a measure of the computer time it takes to execute an algorithm. This usually is a function of the amount of data processed.

Encryption of data   changing the symbols that represent data to other symbols so as to encode it. Unless the secret of decoding is known noone can understand it.

End-of-file value   a special symbol stored automatically at the end of any file of data.

Enter   a term also used for the return key of a keyboard.

Error message   output from the system to inform the user that an error has occurred. The type and location of the error is given in the message.

Exact divisor   an integer that divides a number evenly with no remainder.

Execution   the operation of a program after it has been translated.

Expert system   an application program that simulates the behavior of an expert in a narrow field in providing answers to questions posed by the user.

Exponent   the integer that gives the position of the point (binary or decimal) to accompany another number that gives the actual sequence of significant digits.

Exponential algorithm   an algorithm who execution time rises in proportion to a power that is dependent on number of items to be processed, for example, 2^N if there are N items.

Exponentiation   raising a number to a power, for example, 2^3.

Field of record   one of the items that make up the record structure. Fields need not all be of the same data type.

Field size   the number of character positions reserved for outputting an item.

Forgiving program   a program that asks the user to try again when an incorrect action is taken rather than stopping execution when an input error occurs.

Formal parameter   in the definition of subprograms (either functions or procedures) after the subprogram's name follows, in parentheses, a list of formal parameters each with a colon and a data type after its name. These parameters represent information that is being given to the subprogram for processing or, for procedures, also output that is expected.

Formal relationship   an expression, often mathematical, that relates the unknown in a problem to the knowns.

Format   the layout of information on input or output.

Function   a subprogram that produces a value.

Generalization   expressing a relationship in abstract terms that applies in many particular instances.

Global variable a variable declared in the main program that can be used in any subprogram. In general, it is not advisable to make use of this capability inside the subprogram.

Hardware the electronic and mechanical parts of a computer.

Heuristic principle a principle that may be used to make reasonable guesses about something that cannot be easily calculated or proved.

I/O input and output.

I/O window a window that displays input and output during a program's execution.

Icon a small sketch displayed by the computer. Icons may be pointed to by a mouse and dragged from one place to another.

Index of array the integer that identifies a particular element of an array such as a list. Tables require two index values to identify an element. (Sometimes called a subscript.)

Index of counted loop the integer variable that is set to a value upon entry into the loop and changed on each repetition. The loop it terminated when the index reaches a certain value. The index variable must not be declared or altered in the body of the loop.

Initialization setting a starting value of a variable or values of an array.

Initialization in declaration setting the initial value of a variable or an array in the declaration of its data type.

Input instruction an instruction that causes data to be read into the computer.

Insertion sort a method of sorting where each new entry is inserted in its proper position in an ordered sequence.

Join operator the operator used to join strings together (in Turing the +).

Justified   output that is brought to line up along one edge of the page or screen.

Knowledge base   a systematic grouping of information in machine readable form.

Known   information that is given in the specification of a problem.

Lateral thinking   a technique for helping to solve problems that approaches the problem sideways rather than head on. This novel approach might be productive in some circumstances when the other fails.

Linear search   a technique for looking for a particular item in an unordered list. Each item is examined in turn until the sought for item is found.

List   a sequence of items arranged one after the other.

Local variable   a variable that is defined in a subprogram definition and is accessible only to that subprogram. Variables can be local to loop constructs as well.

Logical operator   an operator that connects two simple conditions so as to create a compound condition.

Lower case   small letters.

Median   the value that divides a sorted list of items in two equal halves.

Menu bar   the screen display of available headings to the menus of individual possible commands in an operating system.

Memory   the part of the computer that stores information.

Merge   to blend two or more sorted lists of items into a single sorted list.

Microcomputer   a computer that is small in size and usable by a single person at a time.

Mixed number   a number that has both an integer and fractional part.

Mouse   a device for controlling the movement of a pointer on the display screen and giving input through clicks.

Mouse button   a device for giving input to the computer by pressing and releasing it.

Multi-way selection   a program construct that selects one of several possible alternatives depending on conditions.

Nested loops   one loop body wholly contained inside another loop's body.

Nested selections   one selection construct wholly contained inside one or other of the alternative clauses of another selection construct.

Operand   the entity that is subject to an operator.

Origin of coordinates   the base point from which distances are measured in the x-and y-directions to locate a point.

Output   information that is displayed, printed, or stored in secondary memory by a program.

Output item   an individual piece of information that is output.

Otherwise clause   the alternative in a case construct that is selected if none of the other labels is matched.

Paragraphing a program   indenting the body of a loop, selection alternative, or subprogram definition beyond the key line that begins the construct.

Pascal   a programming language devised by Niklaus Wirth and widely used to teach computer programming.

Pixel   a dot on the display screen.

Pixel position   the coordinates on the screen of the point where a pixel is located. Each graphics system limits the number of possible pixel positions on the screen.

Pointer   an arrow icon displayed on the screen in response to the positions of the mouse. Also a way of storing the location of a piece of information in the memory.

Polynomial time   an algorithm that is executed in a time proportional to a polynomial in the number of items being processed, for example, N^2+2N+1 if there are N items.

Precedence of operations   the sequence in which operations are performed in evaluating an expression.

Predefined subprograms   subprograms such as *sqrt* that are part of the Turing language.

Prime number   a number that has no other exact divisors but 1 and itself.

Procedure   a subprogram that produces some result when called.

Program window   the part of the display screen used to enter the instructions of a program.

Prompt   output from a program to get the user to take some action such as entering information from the keyboard.

Pseudo-random numbers   a sequence of apparently random numbers that are in fact generated by an algorithm. Each number in the sequence is created from the previous one. The beginning of the sequence is called the seed.

Radix notation   a display of digits in which the position of the digits indicates the power of the number base that is to multiply it.

Random numbers   see pseudo-random numbers.

Read only memory (ROM)   memory used to record information that cannot be changed by the user.

Real number   a number with a decimal point (or binary point). Integers are real numbers but not all real numbers are integers.

Record data type   a data type that permits a group of items of possibly different types, to be treated as a unit.

Recursive merge sort   a method of sorting whereby a list is divided in two and each half sorted by the recursive merge sort and then the two sorted halves merged.

Recursive subprogram   a subprogram that calls itself.

Redirecting input or output   arranging to obtain standard input from a disk file rather than the keyboard or sending standard output to a disk file rather than to the screen.

Redundant information   duplicated information in problem specification, for example, John is 16 and in two years John will be 18.

Related lists   two lists which may be of different data types that are in a one-to-one relationship with each other for example one list of person's names and a related one of their phone numbers.

Relational operator   the operator connecting two items in a condition, for example, in the condition 6 > 5, the > is a relational operator.

Repetition   one of the three basic constructs of all programs. The body of the repetition is to be executed until a condition is met or a counting index reaches a certain value.

Reserved word   either a keyword in the Turing language or the name of a predefined subprogram or constant.

Round off   to change a mixed number to the integer that is nearest to its value.

Run   to start the execution of a program.

Run-time error   an error that is not discovered until execution begins, for cxample, attempting to divide a number by zero.

Saving a file   recording information from memory to the disk (secondary memory).

Scroll the movement of the display of characters on the screen either up or down as a unit.

Search space the number of items of information out of which one particular item is sought.

Selecting a command using a mouse to choose an operating system command from a menu of possible commands.

Selecting text choosing a portion of the display in the program window to be deleted or copied. In some systems this is done by dragging a mouse, in others by marking lines by a command.

Selection one of the three basic constructs that make up all programs. Alternative sets of instructions are selected for execution depending on some condition.

Sentinel a mark or symbol used to indicate the end of a file.

Side effect an action taken by a subprogram that is not its purpose. Functions are not permitted to have side effects in Turing.

Significant digits the string of digits that describe a number without its point (binary or decimal) in its proper place.

Simple condition two expressions separated by a relational operator.

Software computer programs.

Sorting placing a list of items in ascending or descending order of a particular key belonging to the items.

Special character any character other than a letter or a digit.

Spread sheet a display of information often a table used to make projections and financial plans.

Startup disk a disk containing the operating system and compiler necessary to enter and run programs.

Statement the basic elements of a program. See also instruction and declaration.

Step-by-step refinement   a technique for developing a program that moves in steps from a statement of the problem specification in English to a program in Turing to solve the problem.

Step size   the amount by which the index of a counted loop is altered on each repetition.

String   a sequence of characters.

String constant   a sequence of characters contained in quotation marks.

Stub   an incomplete subprogram, generally one with a missing body, used in program development where other subprograms are being tested first.

Subscript   see index of array.

Substring   a portion of a string.

Syntax error   an error in the grammar, or form, of a statement.

Table   a display of values in rows and columns.

Test data   sample data, typical of that which will occur in practice, used to find errors in programs.

Testing a program   running the program using a range of input data typical of what it is expected to process and comparing the output with values obtained " by hand".

Text editor   a program that permits you to change text by deletion, addition, and substitution.

Text processing   changing text both by editing and formatting the output.

Token   a sequence of characters surrounded by white space, that is, blanks or returns.

Token-oriented input   using an instruction that will read text a token at a time.

Tracing execution   carrying out "by hand" the actions that a computer must go through during the running of a program. The values of all variables must be kept track of as the trace proceeds. Used for finding errors that are not syntax errors.

Translation   changing a Turing program into one that can be executed by the computer.

Type definition   a statement in the program that gives a name to a particular non-simple data type, for example, a record type.

Type font   the style and size of a set of characters, letters and digits used for output.

Unknown   the information that is being sought when you solve a problem.

Upper case   capital letters.

User-friendly program   a program that prompts input, labels output, provides help to the user, and often is forgiving when the user makes a wrong entry.

VGA graphics   a commonly used color graphics system for the PC.

Variable   a memory location where information can be stored.

Variable parameter   a parameter of a procedure whose value will be altered by the procedure.

White space   blanks or return.

Window   an area on the screen (possibly the whole screen) where certain kinds of information appear.

Word processor   application software used to enter text, edit it, format it, save it, and so on.

Index